TOWARDS
CASCADIA

Lori,

Thank you for your support!
I hope you and Michael
are enjoying the empty
nest back in Hopkinson.
Best wishes and enjoy
the book!

Ryan

TOWARDS
CASCADIA

Why We Are a Unique Region,
a Society in Need of a New Future,
and How to Achieve it Peacefully

Ryan C. Moothart

CONTENTS

Towards Cascadia | towardscascadia.com

All of the images and quotes in this book meet one or more of the following criteria:

1. They are used with permission from the original author and/or publisher.

2. They are licensed under the creative commons for adaptation and use beyond the creator's original source.

3. They are an original creation of the author.

The reference notations in this book are formatted as follows:

Citations are marked numerically at the end of a clause or a sentence. The corresponding work can be found at the end of this book. Footnotes are marked numerically in superscript where necessary.

ACKNOWLEDGMENTS

A VERY SPECIAL thank you to each of the following (in no particular order):

David McCloskey of the Cascadia Institute (cascadia-institute.org), for his work over the past four decades mapping the geography of Cascadia and allowing me to use his map in this book.

Peter Berg and the Planet Drum Foundation (planetdrum.org), for his work defining bioregionalism, the foundation's work to keep his vocation alive, and the foundation's permission for me to use a quote from Peter Berg's essay, "Reinhabiting California."

Alexander Baretich, for designing the Cascadia flag, selflessly promoting the ideals behind it, and encouraging its wide use across the region.

Douglas Todd, Ronsdale Press, and the many authors of *Cascadia: The Elusive Utopia*, especially Jean Barman, Sally McFague, Patricia O'Connell Killen, and Mark Wexler, for their work and the publisher's permission to use a recreation of one of the book's images, along with several other quotes. Without this book, I would have never been inspired to write mine.

Devin Hess, Mel Sweet, and Casey Bryan Corcoran for their documentary film *Occupied Cascadia*, which gave me valuable insight and direct inspiration for certain parts of this book.

Patricia O'Connell Killen, Mark Silk, and AltaMira Press, for their book *Religion & Public Life in the Pacific Northwest: The None Zone*, and the publisher's permission to use a quote.

Matthew Kaemingk and the Christ & Cascadia blog (christandcascadia.com), for permission to quote a piece from one of his blog posts.

Colin Woodard, for his book *American Nations*, the many insights on American regionalism I gained, and permission for me to use his map in this book.

Joel Garreau, for his book *The Nine Nations of North America*; his unique perspective on American regionalism, which helped inspire me; and his group's permission to use his map in this book.

Patch Perryman, for his keen eye and his permission to use one of his photographs in this book.

The unnamed or anonymous authors of quotes and license-free images that I use in this book.

CascadiaNow! and their work promoting regional coherence, distinction, and pride.

Anyone, past and present, who has found inspiration in the idea of Cascadia to work towards a better, accepting, and sustainable future.

A personal thank you to each of the following (in no particular order):

Friends who have given me feedback and/or encouragement during this project, especially Alyssa Anderson, Kristen Bennett, David Bernstein, Joe Gruber,

Paul McKean, Casey Sparks, Behzod Sirjani, and Maggie Williams.

My husband, Paul, for his constant support, love, and putting up with me in general.

Willamette University and the numerous professors who taught me how to think and analyze the world in a variety of different ways, especially Jeanne Clark, Catherine Collins, David Gutterman, and Cynthia Willis-Chun.

The community at University Lutheran Church in Seattle, for giving my husband and me spiritual grounding and support.

Portent, Inc., and the many people I've had the privilege of working with, especially Ian Lurie, Elizabeth Marsten, Mike Fitterer, Michael Wiegand, and Tracy Beach.

1. INTRODUCTION

THERE IS A scene and setting I believe is more profound and beautiful than anything else in the world. I noticed it the first morning after moving into a new apartment in Seattle a few years ago. I woke up early, after a long day of travel and moving heavy boxes. My new apartment building sat atop a steep hill, overlooking Seattle's historic Pioneer Square neighborhood. My unit had large windows facing west out onto Smith Tower and the Puget Sound. That morning, I walked into my new living room and looked out my windows. I had a crystal-clear view of the Olympic Mountains across the Sound. The gaps in the clouds were dispersing the morning sunrise in a majestic pattern that accented the landscape perfectly. It was as if God himself — or Mother Nature herself—had planned this scene as the most stunning welcome I have ever experienced. I remember staring at this serene and picturesque view, losing my sense of time, and forgetting all of my logistical concerns about moving to a new city. I knew immediately I had found the sense of place I will forever call home. Each time I look out onto those mountains, they provide me with a sense of wonder and clarity. Each time I recall my first morning taking in their view, I remember the feeling of hope and tranquility they provided me.

I am not the first person to have such an experience in Seattle—or in any other locality in this region of the continent—and I am surely not the last; I daresay this type of experience is commonplace here. It's a powerful phenomenon that has shaped the experiences of just about everyone who lives here and even those who visit. It's a phenomenon that forces you to pay attention to the natural beauty that surrounds you and to admire all that stems from it. And it's a phenomenon that permeates throughout the culture of this great region.

The area known to most as the Pacific Northwest is coming into its own; a relatively vibrant, ample, and distinct environment of temperate forests and rain encapsulates an equally distinct society of people. We—the people who call this region home—are unquestionably different from the rest of the continent. We, along with those who came before us, have distinguished this region's identity rapidly over the past few decades, in the context of modern history. It was once an area where indigenous tribes lived off the land, protected it, utilized it, and replenished it. It then became an area where transplant Americans and Canadians settled to "tame the West" under the foolish and destructive philosophy of manifest destiny. Now, it's an area where its people are once again embodying its true nature. Individuals and communities, simultaneously different and alike, are living with devotion to this region and all it has to offer. We have disassociated ourselves, culturally and politically, in exceptional ways from the rest of the continent. And to some of us who have realized this, our region goes by a different name: Cascadia.

Cascadia was created as a sociological identity for the region to describe its unique culture and geography. While it often refers to Oregon, Washington, and British Columbia, the three main entities that make up the Pacific Northwest, it also pertains to Idaho, southeast Alaska, western Montana, and Northern California. The idea's essence has sparked dreams of sustainability, liberty, and progress for the region and its people by those few who have explored the true nature of their surroundings. And such dreams have remained peculiar in Cascadian society—whimsical and merely intriguing—until now.

Something is happening in Cascadia. As ordinary as that sounds in the context of a vague occurrence unimportant to our daily existence or our purpose in life, I mean it as anything but that. "Something," a word used in place of a specific or clear idea, does not necessarily connote insignificance. That "something" is, I believe, becoming incredibly significant. A force, not yet clearly defined, is influencing some of us in Cascadia in ways we can't yet fully comprehend. Many of us don't feel this force and aren't acutely aware of it yet. But a few of us have let it work its influence, and we yearn to help the rest of us feel it. Curious citizens are linking up on social networking sites to discuss what it means to be Cascadian and why it feels important. Activists are gathering in small chapters across the region to foster ideas for improving and raising awareness of it. The Cascadian flag has become a noticeable presence, from major sporting events to retail shops to car bumpers in Portland, Seattle, and Vancouver. Academic-themed conferences and cultural festivals have begun to be held annually to explore and celebrate different aspects of the Cascadian identity.

I've been moved by this omnipotent force and have spent some time exploring its nature. This exploration has given me many ideas I feel compelled to prescribe and share with my fellow Cascadians; hence, my reason for writing this book. So I say again, something is happening in Cascadia. But a more apt phrase for what I'm trying to communicate may be that *something is beginning in Cascadia*; a social movement, more cultural than political, is converging to both explore this newfound yet anciently grounded identity and make a human argument for its distinction. From the native tribes that have inhabited this land since long before immigrants arrived, to the community activists, public servants, and countless business organizations founded here today, we have strived to utilize the best parts of our individual drive and communal interdependence to achieve great things. Now, in our current time of trial, a few of us have come to realize we're going to need to exemplify our distinctiveness again, on levels never before seen, to lift ourselves up and progress towards a more stable future. Small pockets of advocates throughout the region, in both the United States and Canada, have banded together to raise awareness of this fact. A movement that recognizes no arbitrary borders and promotes a new philosophy for the future is growing.

About forty years ago, American ecologist and California counterculture icon Peter Berg helped define a new eco-political concept called *bioregionalism*. This idea has stirred the minds of some environmental and political activists in Cascadia. He stated:

> A bioregion refers both to a geographical terrain and a terrain of consciousness—to a place and the ideas that have developed about how to live in that place. Within a bioregion the conditions that influence life are similar and these in turn have influenced human occupancy.[1]

Geographically, the Cascadian bioregion (defined by ecological traits and the watershed regions of the Columbia and Fraser Rivers) stretches from Northern California to southeast Alaska, from the Pacific Coast to the Canadian Rocky Mountains. While these ecological boundaries are intrinsic components for applying bioregionalism to Cascadia, it's the idea behind bioregionalism as a theory that's at the heart of the movement that's beginning to take hold here. We live in a particular region with a particular environment that has produced—or at least helped influence—particular cultures, philosophies, and ways of life. This idea is also the foundation for the theory that our systems of economy, governance, and interdependence should be based upon the natural, where such environmentally-defined regions are free and sovereign political entities; the civic systems within them based upon regional, locally assorted principles, cultures, and philosophies.[2] And I specify local assortment to iterate that such transcendental elements (culture, et al.) within a bioregion can be diverse but are ultimately compatible because they originate, in part, from the same bioregion within which they exist.

That being said, the theoretical foundation for bio-regionalism is not entirely undisputed. Opinions differ on how, exactly, bioregionalism works; some hypothesize that within a given region, nature is the ultimate determining factor of how culture and identity are expressed, while others say nature merely sets limitations on or corresponds with its analogous culture and identity. Such premises are analyzed, deconstructed, and debated among academics and common citizens and likely will be for the foreseeable future. I can claim without hesitation, however, that bioregionalism will play a significant role in Cascadia's immediate future. Not only is it currently the theoretical keystone to small but significant activism that has already begun propagating awareness of Cascadia as an idea, but it can and will be built upon, including in this book, to transform this movement from a niche and localized phenomenon to a widespread shift in thought throughout the greater Cascadian zeitgeist.

We are unique. Our culture, our politics, our economy, our history are all unique because we live in a different environment from the rest of Canada and the United States. And when I say environment, I'm not just talking about our ecosystems, albeit those are essential parts. We live in a place in which all aspects of it have derived from its environmental context. Our attitudes, daily routines, shared history, social norms—the framework for our society is grounded, at the most basic point of our foundation, in the region in which we live. How different would our lives be without the snow-capped mountains towering in the background of almost every point of our region? How different would our lives be without the Pacific Coast from which our temperate weather arrives? How different would they be without our evergreen forests, our resilient wildlife, and our pristine water sources? What would our towns look like? What would our cities look like? Across the entire Cascadian region and across international borders, our intrinsic ethos is and has been sculpted on the same regional dais; our identities are shared athwart it. Across diverse ancestral backgrounds, innate characteristics, local cultures, languages, and affiliations, we are, essentially, one people.

Cascadia's people are not identified by any ethnicity, religion, or political ideology; we're a very diverse group in just about any characteristic you can name. But the cultural foundation that permeates each of us is a uniting force, whether we are relatively new to the region or have lived our entire lives here. Even within each of our locally unique traditions and ways of life, our outlook on the world in which we live is common. We're largely tolerant of others who are different from ourselves, and we're willing to explore the backgrounds of other cultures, whether or not we subscribe to any strict adherence of organized religion or personal philosophy. We're defensive of our basic human liberties, whether we're politically inclined to be more individualistic or more communal. We love our beautiful natural surroundings and have a desire to protect them and do them justice, whether we're avid outdoor recreationalists, natural resource workers, or just admirers of a spectacular view. These character traits belonging to society at large can be observed in communities across Cascadia. The answer as to why we are the way we are is no mystery. Our cultural foundation, our communication with others, our upbringing—all of it is influenced by the environment in which we live. All of it is persuaded, in part, by our bioregion. Our lush, plentiful, and temperate surroundings are prime conditioning for the very culture we experience on a daily basis. If we go back to the people and communities who inhabited this region long before us, we find evidence of a network of indigenous tribes that flourished on interdependence, shared resources, communication with one another, and peaceful cooperation, regardless of their differences.[3] Today, Cascadia is an interdependent web of diverse cities and townships that espouse similar qualities and characteristics of its native ancestors, even after two centuries of Western influence and the developments of modern technology. To put it simply, our distinct environment directly affects our distinct culture as a society, and our regional culture directly influences our systems of cooperation.[i] It is, therefore, that such systems are both compatible throughout our region—across local particularities and international borders—and fundamentally different from other regions' accumulation of culture.

It should come as no surprise, then, that many are frustrated with our current condition of politics on a federal level in both the United States and Canada. Whether we consider ourselves a Democrat, Republican, Independent, Liberal, Conservative, Green, New Demo-

---

i   Politics, economics, et cetera.

crat, anarchist, or something else entirely, we feel that something is fundamentally off with our political statuses quo in Ottawa and Washington, DC—incompatible with the way we live our lives in Cascadia. And while our economic standing has recovered to an extent from the near-catastrophic collapse less than a decade ago, the unity we're supposed to share throughout our respective countries continues to dissipate in spite of this.

In the United States, polarization has hit its most potent position since the Civil War[4]; the ability to truly compromise in Congress has severely diminished, seen as a sign of weakness instead of a noble gesture on behalf of the interests of the many. Out of fear and vulnerability since the terrorist attacks on September 11, 2001, perpetual warfare in the Middle East continues with no clear mission, and the United States government continues to allot more tax dollars to war than the next ten highest-spending countries combined.[5] All the while, education standards continue to decline for the country's youth[6] and homelessness continues to be at stubbornly high levels since the Great Recession.[7] Elected officials on both sides of the aisle, while well intentioned, are continually swept into a corrupt system that bends to the will of special interests and the few most-wealthy individual citizens in the country.

The United States was once a country where its uniting factors were greater than its dividing factors; this is no longer the case. The United States is not—and really has never been—united in identity. It is seldom capable of uniting in purpose anymore, for this requires a majority to acknowledge and accept more than one way of thinking, which is discomforting for too many. In the past, the citizenry was able to recognize a bold idea and try something new for the sake of progress and the betterment of society. Now, bold ideas are attacked on ideological grounds from both sides of the aisle for not being in line with their philosophies. Wealthy donors fund advertising campaigns designed to aggravate the ill-informed for the purpose of drowning out reasonable discourse, helping to ensure political victory for whatever side such an instance happens to benefit. With such a corrosive atmosphere present in federal politics, people in each region have developed exclusive identities of what it means to be "American" to solidify their beliefs and convince themselves of a clear direction in which the country needs to go, which further divides entire regions of the country.

In Canada, a country that has never possessed as forceful of an identity as its neighbor to the south, citizens from Newfoundland to British Columbia continually struggle with a sense (or lack thereof) of national belonging and distinctiveness. While Canada's parliamentary system of government is inherently more responsive and representative of the Canadian people, communities in Vancouver feel no more connected to communities in Toronto or Montreal than they do to communities in Chicago or New York, except by definition of arbitrary international borders.[8] Quebec, a recognized nation within Canada,[9] has long desired to be more autonomous than other regions of the country and has worked to exercise its influence over the federal government. While the Bloc Quebecois—the federal political party devoted solely to Quebec's interests—is not as strong in Canadian Parliament now as it was at the height of its power in the mid-1990s, citizens outside of that province tend to feel as if Quebec's clout has unduly shifted the balance of political power towards itself at the expense of the other provinces. In recent years, Canada's federal government has begun taking advantage of the West's portion of natural resources for the purpose of multinational corporate profiteering, with minimal input from the citizens whose ecosystems will be permanently affected. The federal government continues to try to authorize oil drilling and pipeline construction from Alberta through British Columbia, among the nonpartisan opposition from the citizens of British Columbia.[10] [11]When man-made disasters do strike, they wreak havoc on the local ecosystem, killing entire communities of plant and animal life and leaving First Nation groups with nothing but the disastrous end-results.[12] This has left many citizens jaded and doubtful they can do much of anything to force the federal government to serve their interests anytime soon.

The problems we as Cascadians face in the United States and Canada are rooted in our fundamental regional differences. They result in the imbalance of power towards our current federal systems, which has led to exclusionary ethics, perpetrated by the most privileged and powerful, and the squandering of opportunity. They result in the corrupt desire of some to unduly impose such ethics on the rest of country as a means of solving the problems that face us. They result in nonresponsive federal representation and an inability to adapt to a more sustainable way of life or a more efficient system of cooperation. Each of these is directly contrary to our collective Cascadian identity. We are out of balance, geographically and fundamentally, as countries; the outcome of this imbalance stares us in the face every day. The recovery from our most recent economic downturn is being held back by the limits of our current federal institutions of power, which have attempted and failed to enact universal solutions on two countries assembled from particular regions. Our solutions for prosperity and tranquility in Cascadia and how our society will subsist afterward can, should, and will be different from the rest of the continent.

We can't force balance on our two countries as they exist currently, but we do know how to restore balance in Cascadia. Between those who value freedom as a more collective principle and those who value it as a more individualistic principle, we, as Cascadians, recognize the interdependence inherent in our region. Cascadians opposed to the use of federal power in the United States and Canada aren't inherently opposed to collective action on more local levels. The answer to solving the issues that face us on their essential levels so we make true progress is not purely individualistic in nature, nor is it purely collective in nature. It's a balance between the two, a new understanding of freedom. Such an answer is directly evident from our innate identity and culture as a region. Our answer is to connect as a region and to engage in these issues our way—the Cascadian way. Then and only then will we be able to progress beyond our current limitations and move forward with securing a better future and a better world for ourselves and all those who come after us.

In order for this to happen, we Cascadians must organize and be willing to come together, despite differences of opinion and thought on contemporary political issues, to unite our region of Cascadia. And I speak of unison not solely in the sense of geography or political entities but unison behind the common objective of Cascadia—self-determination. We desire to establish the foundations for a society where each person has liberty from undue burdens imposed by an inadequate state or an overbearing majority. We desire freedom of opportunity, creating a system of interdependence that allows *each* of us to maximize our own potential. We desire to build and secure a clean, sustainable environment on which we can rely for generations to come. We desire open, honest communication throughout society for the sake of proper engagement and cultivation of our intellect. And these are all objectives that can be achieved peacefully through our democratic processes, as I will elaborate in detail later on. These are not objectives based upon strict ideology or jingoism; they are all-inclusive and able to be adapted by all in our region who wish to seek them. Be you native or newcomer, urban or rural, left or right, religious or atheist, or any classification of the niche labels by which we seem to categorize members of society, you can be *Cascadian* in this region.

I am Cascadian—I have come to realize this to be a good and true fact. Not only am I lucky enough to call this place home, but I also have examined my surroundings and evolved my political consciousness past the indiscernible walls that are raised by the current federal paradigm of our political and cultural reality. This book serves as a testament to my civic beliefs and a guide for any who share these sentiments in Cascadia. In this book, I hope to achieve three things:

1. Help justify the greater movement for Cascadia.

2. Define a clear, tangible goal we can work towards.

3. Empower the citizens of this region to take sensible action.

I do not have the answers to achieve utopia, and I cannot predict what will happen in popular culture or current events that will facilitate our movement's growth organically. I do, however, have a bold idea on what our shared foundation is and how to achieve a new future for Cascadia, which I look forward to sharing with those of you hoping for a new approach.

Cascadia is not my idea; it's a symbolic convergence that has the potential to move the mountains of mainstream thought. It's a dormant reality waiting to be discovered and ascertained. The ideas in this book are not all mine; I have analyzed the writings of others on the subjects that concern us, and I will attempt to coalesce them into a coherent argument that has the fidelity necessary for a popular movement to grow. For all my arguments that follow, I say as a Cascadian for Cascadia and only for Cascadia. By realizing our own potential and truly being Cascadian, we can bring clarity and hope to not just ourselves but anyone who looks to us for inspiration. I wish for a tranquil future in which I and everyone else can live the purpose we were meant to epitomize. I am Cascadian, and I'd like to share this vision with you.

2. OUR UNIQUE REGION AND IDENTITY

WHAT EXACTLY IS Cascadia? What is its identity? What does it mean to be Cascadian? These are the pertinent questions that need to be answered to the best of our ability before exploring any possibilities that may stem from them. Many in this region—perhaps you, reading this now—know their town or city, know their neighbors, and cherish the place they call home, but they don't necessarily see any correlation or connection with those who live in another part of their own state or province, let alone their own region, beyond the simple coincidence of geography. They may realize their immediate surroundings and admire them, but they don't give too much thought to how the continuity of such surroundings throughout a vast region may connect them with someone hundreds of miles away, *beyond* the simple coincidence of geography. We live in a unique, coherent region of our beloved planet with a firm foundation for culture and identity. These can be seen expressed in many ways throughout this region, which are simultaneously different and akin. We have the foundation and the ability to come together, strengthen our interdependence, and advance as a single society that embraces its own true identity. If we wish to come into our own as one unified society, coming together from each fraction of this region, we must recognize that we are indeed one nation of people.[i] We need to discover who we are as one nation, who we've been as one nation, and who we're meant to be as one nation.

This begs the question once again: what exactly is Cascadia? Cascadia is the essence of the Pacific Northwest. It is the name of the region of our North American continent, which spans from the Canadian Rocky Mountains in British Columbia, western Montana, and Idaho, to the Pacific Ocean, and from the temperate forests of Northern California to the islands that make the up the southeastern panhandle of Alaska. It is named after the Cascade Mountain Range, which towers over the land in western Oregon, Washington, and British Columbia and is commonly referred to as the "Pacific Northwest." It is defined geographically by the land that is encompassed by the rivers in the Columbia and Fraser watershed regions, which drain into the Pacific Ocean, as well as the

---

i "Nation" refers to the idea of nationhood, a society based on the public or political beliefs according to the common culture and shared experiences of the place such a society inhabits. This is separate from the concept of "statism" (i.e., "country"), which is the belief that an autonomous political entity should have some degree of control over the public policy of a society. Often times in the United States and Canada, we use the terms "nation" and "country" interchangeably, as if they both meant the same thing. It is vital to realize these two concepts are separate. In many cases around the world, nations are states/countries as well. This is *not* the case for the United States and Canada; I argue these two countries are made up of many nations, as I will elaborate upon in detail throughout the following sections of this book.

similar mountain ranges that exist within the region itself and/or constitute its eastern and southern borders. On page 19 is a visual representation of the region we're exploring.[ii]

While its recognition and legitimacy comes from a designated area of land defined by mountains and rivers, Cascadia is much more than that. Cascadia's unique physical features and placement on this Earth provide for a unique climate. Its abundant natural resources provide for unique ways of life. Its rich history helps solidify its identity. And its people have proven to be pioneers of progress in the evolution of society since before its "discovery" by European settlers.

Cascadia has an ethos—an overarching sense of character regarding its guiding beliefs and ideals, much greater than any narrow set of ideologies—like none other anywhere in the world. It's an ethos of openness, honesty, interdependence, ingenuity, and creativity that has persevered for hundreds of years. It's an ethos that has withstood adversity, misunderstanding, and prejudice, which has led to regrettable actions by select groups of people unto others. It's an ethos that permeates the region and its entire people, across local diversities and particularities. And, most important, it's an ethos that is capable of being exemplified by each of us, even if we don't fully realize it yet. This ethos is our collective soul—the very essence of who we are as a people. Being Cascadian is much more than just living here; being Cascadian means

---

ii   Image Credit: David McCloskey © 2014 (cascadia-institute. org). Used with permission from David McCloskey.

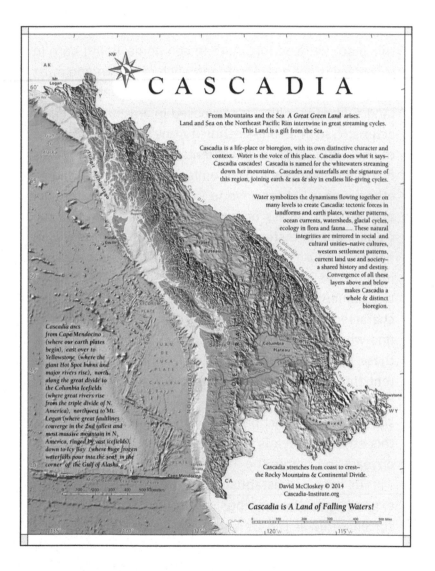

CASCADIA

From Mountains and the Sea *A Great Green Land* arises.
Land and Sea on the Northeast Pacific Rim intertwine in great streaming cycles.
This Land is a gift from the Sea.

Cascadia is a life-place or bioregion, with its own distinctive character and context. Water is the voice of this place. Cascadia does what it says– Cascadia cascades! Cascadia is named for the whitewaters streaming down her mountains. Cascades and waterfalls are the signature of this region, joining earth & sea & sky in endless life-giving cycles.

Water symbolizes the dynamisms flowing together on many levels to create Cascadia: tectonic forces in landforms and earth plates, weather patterns, ocean currents, watersheds, glacial cycles, ecology in flora and fauna.... These natural integrities are mirrored in social and cultural unities–native cultures, western settlement patterns, current land use and society– a shared history and destiny. Convergence of all these layers above and below makes Cascadia a whole & distinct bioregion.

Cascadia arcs from Cape Mendocino (where our earth plates begin), east over to Yellowstone (where the giant Hot Spot burns and major rivers rise), north along the great divide to the Columbia Icefields (where great rivers rise from the triple divide of N. America), northwest to Mt. Logan (where great faultlines converge in the 2nd tallest and most massive mountain in N. America, ringed by vast icefields), down to Icy Bay (where huge frozen waterfalls pour into the sea) in the corner of the Gulf of Alaska.

Cascadia stretches from coast to crest– the Rocky Mountains & Continental Divide.

David McCloskey © 2014
Cascadia-Institute.org

Cascadia is A Land of Falling Waters!

embodying this ethos. "Cascadian" is the state of mind and body that thrives in this region and causes each of us who embrace it to realize our surroundings and cherish this place we're so fortunate to call home. Being born in this place is not a requirement; each of us can and must explore this identity, whether or not we're native to this land. Being Cascadian is not based in any outward characteristic, such as one's ethnicity, one's gender, the color of one's skin, one's sexual orientation, one's religious affiliation, or one's socio-economic standing; the Cascadian ethos is possible for anyone in this region to exemplify and personify in his or her own way. "Cascadian" is the culmination of distinguishing attributes that this region naturally infuses within its inhabitants. Its ethos is based in nature as its very essence. In this section, we're going to examine this ethos and identify these distinguishing characteristics. Or to put it another way, we're going to find what makes "us" us. We're going to understand that these distinguishing characteristics are indeed consistent throughout this entire region, across international borders, and regardless of any specific area's population size or local distinction. And we're going to realize that this ethos we seek is the same now as it was hundreds of years ago, before the influence of western settlement.

To help me establish this, I will paraphrase and expand upon the writings of Dr. Jean Barman, professor emeritus at the University of British Columbia and a leading expert in the history of the Cascadian region. Before the voyage of explorer Juan de Fuca in 1592, or of James Cook and George Vancouver some two hundred years later, the region of Cascadia had been home to several prominent native tribes that laid claims throughout the land, both west (coastal) and east (interior) of the Cascade Mountain Range. Most of these tribes still exist and continue to be strong social influences in Cascadia, whether we as individuals are members of one or not. They each had their own local distinctions, customs, and language(s), which, while diverse and differentiated from one another, were cultivated from a history of living off the Cascadian land. The specifics of these tribes may be unique, but the foundation for their ways of life was the same unifying force. The driving purpose behind each tribe's self-determination was to live in harmony and in balance with nature. This was realized through the common philosophy that oneself and community needed to be inhabitants and stewards of the land they lived off, instead of simple occupants with no responsibility or foresight for the region in which they made their home. The entire region, with the exception of inhospitable or difficult-to-reach areas, was entrusted to and by native tribes. Within a tribe's determined geographic area came the responsibility for its natural resources. It was a tribe's duty to look after its resources, utilize them as needed, and protect them from overconsumption. Furthermore, it was a tribe's duty to give back to the land that provided them with the necessities of life, respecting it and preserving it for generations to come.[13]

Naturally, the land was also a source of spirituality, in which this self-determination was experienced and expressed. The pristine and overwhelming surroundings constituted a medium for religious experience and ritual, while the importance of community—the interdependent network of individuals who worked for themselves and each other—provided for the expression of how spirituality was actualized in daily life. This is the essence of conservation and sustainability—concepts of utilizing resources in a manner both wise and methodical so that we, as communities through individual action unified in spirit, are able to get what we need from the region we live in and ensure its preservation and continued existence for our children, our grandchildren, and beyond. These were and still are common and unifying characteristics throughout this region. We see them expressed today in nearly every locality throughout Cascadia, by both indigenous and non-indigenous communities alike, as principles of common purpose. They may have been expressed differently four hundred to five hundred years ago, but conservation and sustainability were the tenets of daily life within each tribe throughout this region.

Native tribes may have been united in purpose, but that is not to say they were all the same. Each tribe, as previously mentioned, had its own customs and language(s). One might think that such language and cultural barriers would discourage communication and cooperation, but the reality was the exact opposite. Those who have studied these languages hypothesize they were part of a common family, deriving from a single root language that spread throughout the region over time.[14] Even with this differentiation, their common outlook and perceived purpose made it possible for communication, cooperation, and interdependence to thrive within Cascadia. Complex and systemic trading relations flourished and allowed for diverse local economies. The entirety of the region was well traveled, as members of one tribe frequently visited others. While history shows that conflict did sometimes erupt between certain tribes, the region was far more stable, cooperative, and advanced politically than many other regions in North America during the same time period.[15] Such a system of interdependence was evidenced by some of the first European visitors to explore Cascadia by land in the mid- to late 1700s:

> The journals of the first outsiders to cross the Pacific Northwest by land make an important point attesting to indigenous peoples' familiarity with the region far more generally than their own small piece of it. Alexander Mackenzie, the first to do so, recounted how a local man "depicted the lands of three other tribes, in succession, who spoke different languages." Indigenous people assured him that "the way is so often travelled by them that their path is visible throughout the whole journey" and, indeed, Mackenzie was able to follow well-marked trails as he made his way to the coast.[16]

Even through localized differences, interdependence throughout the region thrived. Exemplified through trade and travel, Cascadia was truly one contiguous and coherent region with a balance that was universal in the realms of human interaction and purpose. This unity in rationale and cooperation allowed for a healthy social atmosphere that was optimal for progress. Complex trade and economy allowed for the opportunity in such an atmosphere to develop advanced and distinct methods of utilizing and preserving the region's natural resources; ingenuity and creativity used to enhance daily life were staples of native culture. By the time European settlers began arriving to Cascadia in the late 1700s and early 1800s, this web of native tribes had adapted and evolved more effectively than any other network of such people on the continent. More languages, more localized customs, more trade, and more advanced methods of utilization derived from this region of North America than any other; slightly differentiated from one another but all native to this region.[17] These are illustrations of the common ethos that lives in Cascadia.

So how does this history, the character of those in this region before the influence of Western philosophy or manifest destiny, compare to the character of Cascadia today? For more than two hundred years, our region's culture and ideals have been an infusion of native Cascadian and alien influences: transplant Americans and Canadians, along with immigrants from Mexico, Asia, and various other places. After all this time of Cascadia's outward identity reinventing itself, along with the political separation of this region at the 49th parallel,[iii] the ethos of Cascadia lives on as it did hundreds of years ago. While the ways in which it is expressed and recognized have evolved with time, diversity, and technology, the ethos of

---

iii   The border between Canada and the United States.

this place remains intact. Just as the native tribes that took responsibility for each part of this region formed their purpose around the natural, practicing it in both practical and spiritual manners, we lead the way in such practices today for the sake of future generations. We consciously recognize the awesome influence of our natural surroundings—urban, rural, and suburban alike—and have strongly embraced a civil religion of conservation and sustainability across political ideologies. Just as native tribes developed a network of communication, trade, and interdependence with others different from their own, we work together as communities, across state lines and international borders, to expand the potential for opportunity and understanding. From co-ops and nonprofits to small businesses to public institutions, we look to our neighbors for support and growth. Just as native tribes developed advanced methods of utility and diverse languages of complexity, we often take hold of the better nature of our individualism and the strength of our communities, using them for purposes of innovation. Advancements in technology, in business, in methods of energy consumption, in communication, in art, and in philosophy have been fastened in our recent history. We dare to develop a new idea and run with it, a trait fostered by our diversity and sense of understanding that there's more than one right answer to any issue that faces us.

We're not that different from the past inhabitants of this place. Whatever connections to established social structures with which non-native settlers entered this region quickly dissipated and changed. The statuses quo of identity and community that held steadfast elsewhere, even in the United States and Canada, collided with the nature of Cascadia. The statuses quo for these individuals changed and the ethos of Cascadia held firm, unbreakable. Such a process still happens today when others immigrate to this region, and such a process will continue. That is the nature of "place" itself: it molds the actions of individuals, creating ways to struggle and ways to thrive within it.

If Cascadia has this unbreakable ethos based in the nature of this very region that holds to this day, then how do we identify the basis for the cultural characteristics that exemplify it through individuals and communities in Cascadia? In other words, how do we identify the basis for these aspects of human character that remain common throughout this region's history? To do this, I will enlist the assistance of Dr. Mark Wexler, professor of business ethics at the Graduate School for Business at Simon Fraser University, by paraphrasing and building from his writings on Cascadia's "workplace spirituality." We need to examine the nature of the medium in which the collective character of a society is expressed—*human interaction and human activity*. Within any given society or region, centers of such interaction and activity can be understood in terms of work and economy. That is not to say we can understand the nature of character through money; in this sense, economy refers to a system of interdependent forces and firms[iv] that constitute as

---

iv   An economic body that can be made up of an individual or multiple individuals.

vehicles for human interaction and activity in any given society. We need to examine and understand Cascadia as an economic cluster, with corresponding workplace spirituality that helps define Cascadian society. Dr. Wexler defines an "economic cluster" as follows:

> An economic cluster may be thought of in two interrelated ways. First, an economic cluster can be viewed within the notion of an industry: firms which are interdependent and rely upon the same knowledge base, whether they emphasize strategies of competition or co-operation. Second, in regional studies, an economic cluster is a group of firms that develop within and become interdependent with a region and its economic future.[18]

Firms—the mediums for human interaction and activity—rely upon specific information, depending on their industry, and rely upon the region in which they exist. Successful firms that last and prove sustainable in a given region exemplify the workplace spirituality of that region; it defines the firms as much as the firms work to epitomize and define it. Workplace spirituality can be understood as the underlying essence to the macro-level identity within a given economic cluster.[19] This workplace spirituality can thus be understood as a prime example of the ethos that drives such human activity and interaction and, therefore, becomes the inward identity or character of a region. But before we explore what the workplace spirituality of Cascadia is, we must understand the foundation for workplace spirituality and examine its economic forces.

There are four combinations of economic forces to any economic cluster, each with its own corresponding worldview, or common narrative, in which it operates. Successful firms embody different aspects of each combination, but the ratio of the different economic forces in relation to each other that proves to be successful will depend upon the workplace spirituality of that economic cluster. These four combinations have been identified by Dr. Wexler as the planning cluster, the market cluster, the innovative cluster, and the adaptive cluster.[20] It is important to note that in this naming convention, each combination is labeled as its own cluster, but each plays a part in a greater economic cluster—in our case, society within Cascadia—as a whole. The reason for this naming convention is because in either instance—one of the four combinations of economic forces or a physical area in which firms act—we are referring to a grouping of firms (a cluster); one is a theoretical construct, while the other is a practical adaptation. Each combination can be understood in terms of its relation with the two forces that define it—the level of control (or flexibility) and the level of competition (or maintenance).[21] On the following page is Dr. Wexler's visual representation of this economic cluster model.[v]

The first cluster is the planning cluster. Its worldview of regulation, organization, and hierarchy is strong in control but weak in competition. Firms that thrive in this

---

v   This image is a re-creation. Credit for the contents and design within this image belongs to Dr. Mark Wexler. Used with permission from Ronsdale Press.

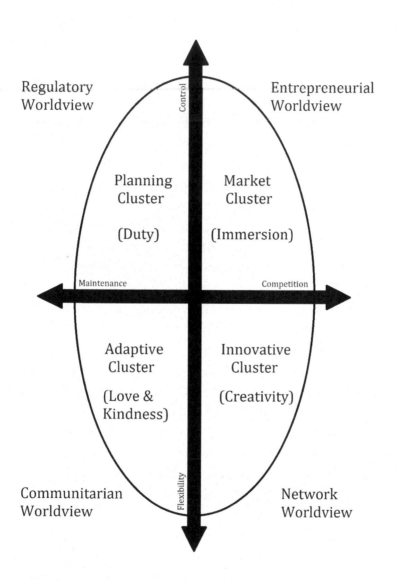

cluster are monopolies that operate for the purpose of maintaining a strong influence and limiting uncertainty, even at the cost of profit. Its corresponding workplace spirituality is that of duty—staying humble, obeying authority, respecting the chain of command, and developing rules/laws for the purpose of maintaining order are key. [22]

The second cluster, going clockwise, is the market cluster. Its worldview of entrepreneurism and profits is strong in both control and competition. Firms that thrive in this cluster are results-oriented and depend upon the strength of individualism, along with the will to beat everyone else. Utilizing one's individual talents to succeed is embraced as achievement through self-realization. Its corresponding workplace spirituality is that of immersion; action—actually doing something and getting direct results—is what achieves success. Planning and discourse can take you only so far. [23]

The third cluster is the innovative cluster. Its worldview of networking is weak in control but strong in competition. Firms that thrive in this cluster depend on the knowledge already available to them and the ability to explore new possibilities to transform that knowledge. Progress and new ideas are the motivating factors for action and success. Its corresponding workplace spirituality is that of creativity, capitalizing on the abilities of individuals to address complex issues, creating something new, and sharing it with the world for the sake of making the planet a better place. [24]

The fourth and final cluster is the adaptive cluster. Its worldview is communitarian and is weak in both control and competition. Firms that thrive in this cluster serve the public good, focus on niche markets, and build a sense of community. Profits are secondary; doing something meaningful and having a purpose for the good of your community is more important. Its corresponding workplace spirituality is that of love and kindness—treating everyone with respect, embracing diversity and those different from you as equals, and creating an environment where you can explore any and all questions.[25]

All four of these combinations of forces exist in some form in any given economic cluster (read: Cascadia) and correspond with a unique workplace spirituality of that economic cluster (read: Cascadia's ethos). Furthermore, this workplace spirituality is understood and practiced within the confines of a particular economic cluster (read: Cascadia); the environment plays a direct role in influencing the development of the firms that exist in it. That regional workplace spirituality is a prime example of the unbreakable ethos that is grounded in the region itself and exemplified through its people.

So what do these economic clusters look like in Cascadia? The planning cluster and the worldview of regulation in Cascadia is undoubtedly the weakest, as compared to the other three clusters and compared to the planning cluster in other regions on this continent. Conventional structures of social order have never thrived here. Take organized religious institutions for example; over 60% of residents in Oregon, Washington, & Alaska consider themselves to be uncommitted to any organized religion.[26] Statistics are similar in British Columbia and

Northern California. The only anomaly in the region is Idaho, where over 40% of residents identify themselves as Mormon. Patricia O'Connell Killen, professor of religion at Gonzaga University, summarizes these trends:

> No single denomination or religious community has been present in any period in numbers sufficient to constitute a dominant public force with which all must contend. This absence of a single, persistently dominant, strongly institutionalized religious reference group colors all individual and institutional religiousness in the region. The region also has a long history of geographic, social, and psychic mobility. Mobility offers options and severs social relationships. In addition, the region's unsurpassed physical grandeur and topographic variety pervade people's experience, overwhelming and awing them. In the Pacific Northwest, topography dwarfs human communities.[27]

This is not to say that we, as Cascadians, aren't religious; many in this region identify themselves as personally spiritual but still claim no affiliation to an organized religion. Why is that? Religion fills a void in the human psyche's need to know the answers to the purpose of our existence. In Cascadia, the notions of morality and understanding our purpose is witnessed and experienced in arguably the most awe-inspiring and powerful natural community of life on this continent. The nature of our surroundings gives each of us that sense of understanding that is commonly provided by organized institutions in other regions. This is why an overwhelming majority of Cascadian residents list their religion as "none." Spirituality is experienced in a more personal way here. Outside of organized religion, authority in general is largely seen as a distant force, one that has little influence here. The need to adhere to a regulatory worldview to limit uncertainty is far less existent. Compared to other regions on this continent, Cascadia lacks socially based laws designed to instill tradition and order. Alternative and/or minority ideas and ways of life aren't viewed as threatening to the majority or plurality that lives differently; individuals are left to their own discretion to live as they choose and empower themselves. This helps explain this region's tradition of decentralized political power, giving local communities a greater opportunity for self-governance. The online blog *Christ & Cascadia*, run in part by the Fuller Seminary Northwest in Seattle, describes this tradition as such:

> Cascadians share a deep devotion to individual liberty as an overriding political good. On the whole, if you are from Cascadia you are either a liberal or you are a libertarian. More liberty is the accepted purpose of political life . . . [Cascadians share] a deep passion for local and direct democracy. Whether on the right or the left, Cascadians tend to bristle at the notion of being controlled by either Washington, DC, or Ottawa.[28]

Any organization that contains an overwhelmingly centralized power structure has little appeal to those in this region. Furthermore, Cascadia's population is so mobile and so unique that the tried-and-tested methods that keep such a centrally organized firm running in other regions do not work here. Thusly, such firms have trouble adapting. Firms can succeed in the planning cluster here, but not many have. Those that do succeed focus on natural preservation as a sense of duty. The importance of sustainability in this way is essential for the maintenance of the regulatory worldview. One could argue, however, that sustainability's significance and presence has less to do with the influence of any regulatory organization and more to do with the fact that sustainability is a part of our regional civil religion, a uniting civic force that gives any collective regulation around this issue legitimacy.

Innovation is arguably the strongest economic cluster in this region. Cascadia has long been known for its strength with embracing creativity, new ideas, and the possibility of great progress, both social and technological. This is the region where firms have blazed new paths in industries such as computer software, green-energy technology, biotechnology, aviation, and agricultural technology. Cascadia largely skipped the industrial/factory phase of economic development and moved quickly to become a service-and technology-oriented economy. This has led to an influx of a higher-educated population with unique skills to ensure these firms continue to thrive. This has also led to a culture where new ideas are met with excitement rather than fear, where new ideas are analyzed and debated on their merits instead of their congruence with the status quo. Seeing as our culture is very much based on the natural, from environmental education to the enjoyment of outdoor activities and everything in between, it's no wonder the innovative ideas surrounding sustainability have succeeded here, engrossed in the minds of our citizenry and championed by such firms that call it their purpose. But it's more than that. Innovation in itself is built upon a worldview of networking—interdependence and shared knowledge. Cascadia's geography and environment have always encouraged more community-oriented population centers rather than sprawling areas of dense population; we've had to be interdependent as communities in order to thrive here. It's these factors and this basis that allows individual development and achievement in the realm of ideas to succeed. Individual creativity thrives because we, as networks of local communities and firms, work together. Firms in different industries and areas of the region are strongly linked throughout it because of innovation. Just like the interdependence and creativity that existed in the native tribes of this region hundreds of years ago, this economic cluster continues to be proven resilient and powerful in Cascadia.

The other two clusters that seem almost diametrically opposed to each other—the adaptive and the market—both have strong roots in Cascadia, operating in the realm of the natural. For both, experiences with nature are personal and thereby meaningful. First, with regard to the market cluster, entrepreneurism succeeds in nature's developed form, creating technologies or services that allow others to take advantage of what this region has to offer. These firms develop land to create resorts and rec-reational areas for our enjoyment of nature. They create environmentally friendly products and construct LEED[vi]-certified buildings for nature's preservation. Acts of con-sumerism are understood as protecting the environment and revering the natural world out of a will for immer-sion, thereby achieving spiritual tranquility.[29] Firms in the market cluster can also succeed in nature's wilderness form by using it as a means for exerting individualism. Cascadia is a place where people can challenge them-selves, survive outside the confines of an urban setting, and learn to improvise in order to conquer the adversity contained in the wilderness. In this cluster, the region is a resource that can be consumed. Just as important, the region is a resource that should be preserved and invested in. The natural landscape left intact and open to all who wish to enjoy it is much more valuable in the long term than permanently destroying it for the sake of a structure designed to appease short-term material gratification.[30]

With regard to the adaptive cluster, communities succeed when living in balance with their surroundings. In the communitarian worldview, nature is the founda-tion for a healthy society. Living in harmony with the land and neighbors that surround you is the key to happiness, tranquility, and self-determination:

> Human communities which act on the natural
> cycle and with the rhythms of nature become less

---

vi   Leadership in Energy & Environmental Design.

drug addicted, less violent and less prone to the exploitation of the marginal, powerless and ill. This occurs because the rhythms of nature, when observed and built into the community, lend themselves to recognition that all of us—rich and poor, men and women, young and old, white, coffee-coloured, and black—join the whale, the badger, the ptarmigan, the river system, the glacial estuary and the weather system as part of the community in nature.[31]

Firms and individuals thrive in this economic cluster when they embrace diversity and recognize that they themselves are not more important or worthy than anyone else in the big picture. These firms act locally to create positive change and effects within their own communities, hoping to both grow the influence of their cause and inspire others to act in the same manner. They are sensitive to new ideas, new ways of doing things, and new technologies—those deemed positive are embraced and used to enhance local communities. Success in the communitarian worldview is achieved through cooperation and symbiotic relationships.

Each cluster exists in Cascadia in certain ways, embracing a workplace spirituality that works in this region in order to thrive. Each cluster is also understood largely in the context of nature here; the massive influence of our natural surroundings forces Cascadians to pay attention and experience their self-awareness in these terms. This phenomenon directly affects how these clusters operate and how firms tend to succeed in the greater economic cluster (read: Cascadia). For example, if we altered our environment, over-consuming our resources and over-expanding our population centers, we would diminish the natural medium in which immersion takes place. We would weaken our ability to exercise individuality and competition in the same manner we currently do in this region, thereby diminishing the market cluster as described in this section and, thusly, altering Cascadia's workplace spirituality. This is one important hypothetical scenario that shows how and why one particular cluster exists in Cascadia as it does. The same rationale of environment affecting workplace spirituality holds true for each combination of economic forces. The combination of these bases for human action and interaction create a unique blend of characteristics that make up Cascadia's ethos.

In Cascadia, the planning cluster is realized through our rational self-governance, where progress can be achieved through a logical, incremental series of steps that are seen as legitimate and recognized as such in this region. This workplace spirituality of duty is most prominently recognized in issues of sustainability and conservation—they are a part of our civil religion, which unites us and gives legitimacy to collective action. Balance, peace, and freedom are only possible if our shared duties and rights are respected. This is the key to a truly sustainable future in which our region is preserved for those who come after us. The market cluster is realized through rugged individualism, where one is able to immerse oneself in all this region has to offer and is able to live in the manner one sees fit. Authority is distant and control is local. Freedom is realized through exercising individual rights without the undue influence of an illegitimate source of control looking to skew the balance of power in its own favor. The absence of coercion by any person or group, thereby allowing an individual to exercise free will and determine his or her own fate, is the key to Cascadia's future. The innovative cluster is realized through creativity, honest hard work, and a network of resources and information. Sincerity and trust are exemplified in order for interdependence to exist. Open communication is the key to progress and the key to a sustainable future. The adaptive cluster is realized through the humbleness of individuals and the resilience of local communities. Diversity is embraced in many of its forms. Acceptance and individuality thrive, creating a region in which no single hegemonic social group establishes a majority. Because of this, new ideas develop and seep into the greater consciousness, allowing progress to ensue. Having each person be accepted as he or she is, thereby allowing each individual to become the master of his or her own fate and maximize his or her potential, is the key to Cascadia's future. *This combination is a prime example of Cascadia's natural ethos.* This is the ethos that has the potential to reside in each of us, stemming from the region we call home.

Individuals have unique personalities and identities of their own, but their actions and interactions are curtailed to adapt to the region in which they live. This ethos represents the way to live and thrive in Cascadia. Its fidelity exists and is maintained because it works and reflects the true nature and reality of this region. It is truly unique, just as the ethos of any other region is differentiated from another. It also holds true across international borders. Whether you reside north or south of the 49th parallel in Cascadia is irrelevant and arbitrary; the common culture and identity of Cascadia is the same in the United States as it is in Canada because Cascadia's environment has a single coherent distinction through-out the entire region. Aside from slight differences in law and politics, the prevailing means of human action and interaction are the same. This is why many, including me, who call Cascadia home feel more commonality with areas of this region they've never visited in the country opposite of the 49th parallel than they do with other areas outside of Cascadia within their own country. There's far less confusion, misunderstanding, and culture clash for an Oregonian or Washingtonian visiting British Columbia than there is visiting Massachusetts, Illinois, Florida, or Southern California. Even when looking at the realm of domestic politics, political parties may be different in the United States and Canada, as well as the federal models of governance in which they operate, but the founda-tions for the political left, right, and middle are the same in British Columbia as in Washington, Oregon, or Idaho. Many strong parallels exist between the stances on is-sues and political philosophies of the state/provincial branches of our political parties when addressing such issues that affect us in Cascadia. This is due to Cascadia's continuity as a congruent, contiguous region, culturally and economically, due to the region's common environmental distinction. In this manner, the political and territorial claims of our two countries matter far less than our shared nature as one nation of Cascadians.

Before either the United States or Great Britain bothered to lay claim to any part of this region, it essentially existed as a single political entity, albeit with no national model of political power. Both countries agreed to joint occupation of the entire area known as the Oregon territory a few years after the War of 1812 ended. The original intention for this territory was not supposed to follow along the lines of what resulted with the naïve and devastating philosophy of manifest destiny—the westward expansion of both the United States and the British Empire. In 1813, Thomas Jefferson wrote a letter to fur trader John Astor after the establishment of Fort Astoria, what was then a trading post in modern-day Astoria, Oregon. In that letter, he wrote:

> I learn with great pleasure the progress you have made towards an establishment on Columbia River. I view it as the germ of a great, free and independent empire on that side of our continent, and that liberty and self-government spreading from that as well as this side, will ensure their complete establishment over the whole.[32]

Ambition and over-zealousness changed that intention rather quickly as the political powers that were in London and the District of Columbia looked to expand their influence in North America. The United States and the British Empire forged westward over the next few decades in an attempt to assert their dominance in an international game of empire-building. The Pacific Northwest territories on the North American continent would be explored and "claimed" by European and American settlers. An "independent empire" never became reality, as the jointly claimed Oregon Territory was divided between the United States and British Empire. A region that had been whole and free was split in two by an arbitrary political border made by diplomats concerned with geographic areas on a map. The two countries agreed on the 49th parallel as the dividing line between American and British territory in 1846, but the Cascadian region and its possibility for unity remained in limbo for the next few decades. On numerous occasions, most notably after the purchase of Alaska from Russia, the United States tried to acquire what became the British Columbia colony. However, those in the colony became disenchanted with the possibility of annexation to the United States and decided joining the new Canadian federation was preferable to attempting to fight for their own independence.[33] In 1870, the border at the 49th parallel between the United States and Canada became permanent, ensuring that the political reality of an unremitting, coherent region was forcibly torn in two. The colonial mind-set of the imperialistic paradigm at that time won out, and Cascadia, in the political sense, remains divided today by an artificial and arbitrary line.

This region was meant to be united as one. We have these qualities and this ethos that makes us distinguishable as a region. We have a vigorous civil religion that flows from the natural elements around us, unlike anywhere else on this continent. Through international borders, our unifying surroundings and economy already give us a sense of network and familiarity, even if so much potential for progress remains dormant. These elements and this identity are not American or Canadian; they're Cascadian. They're unique to us. They are us. Our values, our ways of life, and our civil religion are indeed parallel to those of the United States and Canada, but no longer are they in lock-step; indistinguishable from the ethos of our two countries. Being Cascadian just doesn't feel the same as being American or Canadian anymore. This is not a statement of judgment, and this is certainly not to say that Cascadian is a superior identity. It is simply a matter of fidelity and being true to our reality. In other words, it just is.

The course of events has proceeded through our history to arrive at this point in time where such a realization is inevitable. We have the opportunity to focus on the aspects of Cascadia that truly unite us: our economy, ecology, geography, lifestyle, spiritual practices, and political foundation. We can realize that beyond the international boundaries and diversities in local customs or local distinctions, we truly belong together as one nation. Cascadia, as a whole region, was once a powerful and compelling force, and it has the potential to be so once again.[34]

Cascadia has an identity that takes all that's put into it by its inhabitants—experiences, beliefs, practices, and

other aspects of human interaction and understanding—
and forges this entirety through the crucible of realization
so its conformed and true ethos remains strong. Cascadian is not an exclusive identity of status, nor is it one that
requires a certain subset of surface-level requirements of
class, wealth, education, or innate characteristics, such as
ethnicity or skin color. Cascadian is an inclusive identity
that has diversity and multiculturalism woven into it.
If you experience this civil religion of the natural that
influences our lifestyle, and if you embrace this ethos
that encompasses our way of life, then you are Cascadian,
regardless of where in this region you live, what political ideology you subscribe to, what religion you practice,
what color your skin is, or even where you were born. If
you live here or come to this region in search of a better
future, you have the potential and opportunity to become
and understand what it means to be Cascadian.

What is not yet Cascadian in this region will become
Cascadian over time. A sudden influx of outside influence
may offset this balance temporarily, but such a movement is both unstable and short-lived; the ethos of this
region survives and will continue to thrive in the manner
we recognize, as long as the natural surroundings that
ecologically define Cascadia continue to thrive with it.
As long as we are true to it, Cascadian will never become
an identity of exclusion

This inclusive nature of identity is incredibly important. If we examine how identity has been used as
political force in empires and nation-states throughout
history and even in many countries to this very day, we

will see it has largely been used as an exclusionary means of definition. Too often, it has been wielded by the powerful for the purposes of domination. Cascadian, as we know it today, has been formed on two countries built upon multiculturalism, which makes this identity an anomaly of sorts, compared to most other national or regional identities around the world. While the Cascadian identity requires the distinction of specific geography and environment, such a unifying regional classification of people is a marvel. I believe Cascadia's history and natural strength of inclusion combined with its emerging visibility as a divergent regional identity make us the perfect aspirant to begin walking down a new path towards a new, self-determined future.

3. THE REALITIES AND POSSIBILITIES OF BIOREGIONALISM

I envision a future in which Cascadia is a unified entity once again. I envision a future in which the surroundings we know and love—the surroundings that make this place "home"—flourish and prosper with our help and awareness. I am hugely optimistic that this future is not only possible but realistically attainable in our lifetime. And I know that if we are to attain this future, it will be possible because of the realities of a concept called *bioregionalism*: the system of cultural and political values exemplified by the people of an ecologically defined region, which are made distinctive by the environmental foundations of that region. Bioregionalism is not only the answer to why each ecologically congruent region on this continent has a distinct political and cultural identity; it is also the answer to how we can foster our region's inherent ethos, reconcile our politics, improve our standards of living, and affirm the natural providence of Cascadia.

There are two components to bioregionalism. The first is an ecologic and geographic component that defines a bioregion physically. The second is a philosophical component that defines how a bioregion constitutes a natural ethos. We will explore both components in this chapter—how they've shaped the cultural and political realities we witness today in upper North America and draw upon their possibilities for Cascadia in our immediate future.

In the previous chapter, I defined the physical region of Cascadia as the common area from the Canadian Rockies to the Pacific Ocean and from the temperate forests of Northern California to the southeast Alaska Panhandle. This region wasn't defined as such because it was convenient or looked cool on a map; Cascadia is a bioregion. A bioregion is a large area composed of similar groupings of interconnected ecosystems called ecoregions, which in turn are interdependent and directly connected with one another. A bioregion has similar environmental conditions and characteristics that encompass natural ecological communities—fauna (animal life) and flora (plant life)—distinct to that region, which is bounded by natural elements, rather than artificial, man-made borders. There's no exact or uniform code to determine the specific boundaries of bioregions or the ecoregions that make them up; nature is not so precise, and the outlines of these regions are transitional rather than abrupt. But the physical composition and shape of these regions are agreed upon by the standards of environmental science and ecology. The common geographic and environmental factors in Cascadia have created a region with distinct and parallel natural communities that are shared throughout the region. Its many rivers flow from the snow-peaked mountains and lakes to the Columbia and Fraser watershed regions out into the Pacific Ocean. We—the people who live in this region—are connected by our shared environment, our shared landscape, and our shared natural resources. We breathe the same air, drink the same water, and experience life in the same surroundings. We live on one common, natural foundation that gives us what we need to sustain ourselves through interdependent networks of community and economy.

This is where the philosophical component comes into the equation. Because a bioregion has a coherent and distinct environment, it shapes a coherent and distinct way to live in that environment. This subsequently creates a distinct ethos and sense of identity for that region, which the communities within it embody and espouse through interaction, economy, and value systems. To better understand this concept and how it works, we can apply it rudimentarily to our environment on the most local levels in our daily lives. Think about how you behave and act in your own home. What about the structure itself and the environment it creates causes you to act in certain ways? Does a small water heater prompt you to take quick showers in the morning? Does your lack of a dishwasher cause you to wash your dishes by hand? Does the lack of sufficient lighting create a more subdued ambience? Do the colors of your walls solicit any type of emotions from you? Answering these and other similar questions can help you understand the personified character, or "identity," of your house. Now ask yourself another question: is the way you act and interact in your own home the same as when you enter into your place of work? How about your school or church? How about a bank, a restaurant, a hospital, or a sports arena? What about each of these places causes you to act and interact in distinct ways? What are the respective identities of these places? Each of them creates an environment that curtails the actions of those within it to conform to that place's identity. There's a way to live and thrive appropriately in that place, however the people within it deem, which is sustained by its environment. While the parts of your personal identity—what makes you "you"—always stays intact, you conform your actions to the identity and the foundation of the place you are in. Furthermore, your beliefs about your environment and everything it entails—other people, your surroundings, societal power structures, predominant value systems, etc.—is affected by that foundation and identity of the place you are in. While a place's identity adapts, in part, to people who are in it, there will always be an empirical and unchangeable distinctiveness to a place, thanks to its foundation for identity, which is defined by the physical makeup of that place itself.

This is the same way a bioregion works; the identity and way to live in that region is defined and formed directly, at least in part, by the environmental and ecological components of that place. And even though its outward character adjusts over time to the masses that reside in it, the times in which we live, and the people who immigrate to it, the intrinsic identity and ethos that derives from the land itself perseveres and outlasts any changes in culture or tradition brought to it by alien influences.

For far too long, the popular model of understanding societal identities has been based upon race and ethnicity. Battles are waged over ethnic differences in certain areas of the world to this day. We put stock in our ethnic and racial backgrounds to go beyond the simple purpose of understanding a person's ancestry. We judge and value people based on these characteristics, which are, ultimately, inconsequential. We've done so throughout human history, not because there are inherent differences in people's character based on the pigmentation of their skin or the particular structure of their skeletons, but because these visible differences in people and communities allowed us to label, compartmentalize, and make sense of our reality. In the case of society in the United States and Canada, communities of settlers tended to establish themselves by people coming into community with other people whose customs, culture, and visible characteristics were familiar to them. This is part of human nature—often when put in an unfamiliar situation, we'll gravitate towards others who exhibit signs of familiarity because it makes us feel more comfortable. That is not to say that people who maintained certain cultural traits did so because their skin was a certain color; that's just the visible connection we're often able to make in an attempt to understand other people we don't know personally. Nevertheless, this visible connection has led us to define cultural identities using racial and ethnic differences.

The rational thought process under this model looks like this:

People → Ethos → Circumstance → Outward Action = Identity

By relying on racial and ethnic definitions of people, we link those directly to their guiding principles of character, which influence their methods of acting and interacting with the world around them (e.g., cultural customs, social norms). We then take these actions, and we identify groups of people based upon them. This is why we jump to conclusions and create stereotypes of other people based on limited or no exposure to them. What we completely miss by using this model is how and why these methods of action and interaction were sustained in the first place. Let's use a rudimentary, hypothetical example to help us understand how this model works and what we're ignoring because of it. Let's say you live in a typical suburban town outside of Seattle, and a family from England moves next door to you. You observe them consistently having afternoon tea on their back porch when the weather is suitable. You know this isn't a common trend in the Seattle area, so you link this routine action with this family's cultural background. This is a trait you associate with the English ethnicity, so you may jump to the conclusion that other people you know who are English or have an English background may share the same custom. This line of thinking sounds reasonable. But the underlying assumption we're making in this example is that there's something inherent in English ethnicity—the shade of the skin pigmentation and the shape of the skeletal structure commonly identified as being predominantly English—that leads people to drink tea in the afternoon. Obviously, this is a rather absurd assumption. We know that people don't just follow a given custom or stereotypical expectation because of their race or ethnicity. Each individual has free will and can choose whether or not to follow any given custom or expectation. So why do we jump to these types of conclusions when we know the underlying assumption, which gives this type of rationale fidelity, is false? The answer is, as I alluded to previously, that we link patterns of actions other people make based on what we can observe about the people themselves, such as their physical characteristics. What we completely miss is the concept of "place" and the vital role it plays in sustaining the guiding principles for belief and action, allowing actionable traits to become customary and routine.

Let's go back to the example of a tea-drinking English family. We know afternoon tea is a custom in Britain that many people in that country observe. We also know there's nothing inherent in their physical characteristics that leads or forces them to partake in this custom; people who are ethnically English and others who are not ethnically English often partake in afternoon tea in Britain. So why is this custom a noticeable trait among people in Britain? The answer lies in the concept of "place"; that is, however an actionable trait is introduced in any given society, whatever the circumstance, the ability of that trait to become customary or distinguishable will depend directly, at least in part, on the environment in which that society resides. In this example, there are aspects to the English custom of drinking afternoon tea that are circumstantial; it was introduced as a social action at some point during Britain's history by an individual or group of individuals. The fact that this custom uses tea and not coffee can be traced back to the colonial history of the British Empire. But the fact that the action of drinking afternoon tea became a staple of British society at some point in its history is due to the fact that the environment of the British Isles helped sustain this custom. Would this custom have survived long if Britain was consistently sunny and 110 degrees Fahrenheit year-round, or if water sources were scarce and hard to come by? Perhaps, but these factors would have made such a practice more impractical to become routine.

The point is that "place" plays some sort of direct role in shaping the guiding principles for action and, therefore, identity, in any given society. Using this thought process, the rational model for identity looks like this:

People → <u>Place</u> → Ethos → Circumstance → Outward Action = Identity

Because we don't see or experience the places from which social norms and cultural customs that are foreign to us come, we often ignore this vital key to understanding the concept of identity. This key that is "place" is the reason why we witness people with different types of cultural and ethnic backgrounds adapt to new ways of life in our own towns and cities. We know people who are ethnically "foreign" to North America yet are second-, third-, or older-generation citizens of our respective countries and fit in seamlessly with the dominant ways of life. For that matter, most citizens of the United States and Canada, including me, are ethnically foreign to North America (read: not Native American or a member of a First Nation tribe), yet we have established different social norms and customs from those that exist in our ancestral home countries. If our previous understanding of identity, which excluded the concept of place, was true, then this reality would not be possible. Because of "place" and the role it plays in shaping ethos and actions, people of any ethnic or racial background have the potential to embody the societal ethos that exists in any given environment.

Think of it this way: if people were colorless, genderless stick figures, how would you identify and differentiate societies from one another? You would observe patterns of actions and interactions dominant among these figures in a given area. The differentiation of these dominant patterns would then be subscribed to the environments that support them and not the physical characteristics of the figures themselves. I realize this is an impossible hypothetical situation that cannot be directly tied to our reality as human beings. But the concept remains true—racial and ethnic differences between human beings are only "skin deep," so to speak. The concept of identity can come from these and other characteristics, but I argue the identity and ethos of a society should be rooted in place and environment. This is what makes societies unique and fundamentally different from one another.

For the better part of the past 150 years, the United States has acted as the world's melting pot—a land where foreigners from around the globe could immigrate, fuse their traditions and culture with those that already exist, broaden America's identity, and assimilate to the American way to achieve a wide range of possibilities and become part of the American dream. This mythic narrative still exists today and is a driving force for the countless number of underprivileged foreigners who come to America for a new lease on life. The assumption behind this narrative is the metaphor that the United States, as a whole, acts as a giant melting pot that fuses alien influences with existing traditions and, like a crucible evaporating the impure elements from the concoction, produces a unified national identity. *This assumption is false.* This process of cultural fusion and assimilation does indeed happen in the United States on a consistent basis, as it does in Canada, but not as a whole country. Bioregions, with their unique cultural foundations based in their environments, act as the melting pots in this narrative. It is not that foreigners come to the United States or Canada and assimilate with an American or Canadian ethos; it is that people, both citizens and noncitizens alike, move to a region and assimilate with the ethos of that region, maintained by the environment that shapes it. These regions are the United States' and Canada's true nations, not the federal entities that most people currently call "nations." This is why it is naïve to try to understand the "American people" or the "Canadian people" as a unified entity; in the framework of this metaphor, the United States or Canada is multiple people, not one person. The United States or Canada may be unified by political borders on a map, but our bioregions make us fundamentally different societies within and/or between our respective countries.

This is not a new phenomenon. In fact, I argue this phenomenon stems back to before European settlement ever began on the upper portion of this continent. I would like to illustrate three different periods of time from three different sources, each showing regional differentiation in North American culture and identity.

Prior to England's settlement of Jamestown or the Spanish settlements in the southwest area of what is now the United States, native tribes inhabited upper North America relatively free from outside influence. These tribes used the natural resources at their disposal to create and sustain a society—everything from the clothes they made to the food they cooked to the languages they spoke derived directly from the environment in which they lived. Anthropologists have identified Native American cultural areas in what is now the United States and Canada, regions where the patterns of activities within and between different tribes were relatively homogenous within them. In essence, these areas were used to identify geographic regions where the identities of the different tribes shared a greater common identity. This is where we get the different classification of Native American tribes (e.g., Great Plains, Plateau, Northeast Woodland).

Fast-forward a couple of hundred years; settlers from Britain, Germany, and other Western European countries begin colonizing and settling upper North America's East coast. These settlement groups have radically different social norms and ways of life, compared to the native people who already lived there. Over the next couple of centuries, colonization and immigration explodes, battles are fought, and settlement moves westward, clear across the continent. By the turn of the twentieth century, after a tragic and regrettable history of conquering native tribes and forcibly taking their land and resources, settlement patterns have been established largely based on demographics and culture. Journalist and historian Colin Woodard recently published a book covering this history of settlement and westward expansion according to the regional patterns that emerged from them.

Fast-forward again to the latter half of the twentieth century; globalization has begun, Americans and Canadians are becoming more mobile—moving from one region to another—and technology has begun to boom. Journalist Joel Garreau of the *Washington Post* travels around the continent in the late 1970s and early 1980s to explore the different regional cultures of the United States and Canada. He publishes a book telling the stories of the people he came across, providing an ahistorical snapshot of our countries' unique regions. These three accounts (see page 58) —covering three different periods of time, each with a different focus—have corresponding maps that outline the patterns they find.[i]

---

i   Bottom two images used with permission from Colin Woodard and Joel Garreau (respectively).

Native American/First Nation Tribes & Regional Culture Areas

Prior to 1600 (400+ years ago)

Image Credit: This image has been released by the copyright holder to the public domain and is a representation of several other similar maps outlining Native American culture areas.

Immigration Patterns Among North American Settlers Prior to 20th Century

Approx. 1600 – 1900

Image Credit: Woodard, Colin. *American Nations: A History of the Eleven Rival Regional Cultures of North America.* New York, New York: Penguin Books, 2011.

Ahistorical Snapshot of American Regional Cultures in Late 20th Century

Approx. 1980

Image Credit: Garreau, Joel. *The Nine Nations of North America.* New York, New York: Avon Books. 1981.

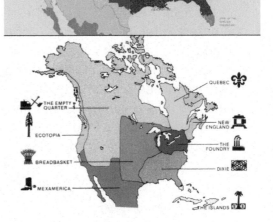

Notice the unmistakable similarities between these three maps. Native American regional cultures, post-settlement/preindustrial regional cultures, and modern-day regional cultures: each has incredibly similar geographic patterns to one another. What are the only factors each account has in common with one another that would lead to these similarities? The answer is the regional geography and environments in which each of these societies lived: North America's bioregions. Allow me to introduce a bioregional map (see following page) and compare it to these other three maps that outline distinctions of regional culture.[ii]

This isn't just a neat coincidence; bioregionalism is the X-factor that holds these patterns together. Just as native tribes adapted to their environments over time to embody the ethos of the region in which they lived, signified by their cultural areas, so did the settlers who immigrated to this continent. Groups from similar areas settled a wide range of land for the purpose of colonization; foreign cultures and systems of values were forcibly inserted into North America's bioregions. But as these foreign cultures and value systems have had time to adapt to their environments, these designated areas have become more noticeable and more prominent. We

---

ii   Bioregional map image depicts upper North America's bioregions according to one scheme. It is not *the* defining map of bioregions; no such map exists, and any created are open to interpretation. This bioregional map is part of the Creative Commons, and no credit has been attributed to the creator. Bottom two images used with permission from Colin Woodard and Joel Garreau (respectively).

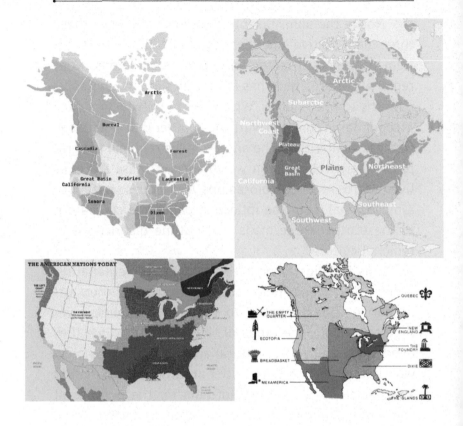

continue this process now; we adapt to our regional environments and embody a distinct ethos that fits it as present-day integrated societies, fused from cultural backgrounds, native and foreign alike.

As a brief aside, I would like to point out two discrepancies between these maps regarding Cascadia, which may lead some to doubt the patterns founded in bioregionalism and thereby doubt the inherent unity of the Cascadian region. First, the map depicting Native American culture areas separates two areas identified as "northwest coast" and "plateau," whereas the bioregional map has these areas united in Cascadia. While anthropologists have made the distinction between northwest coast and plateau, these two areas did encompass tribes from one group—the Salish people—unified through their ethno-linguistic origin.[35] While the Salish are commonly separated by coast and interior, their history of common distinction, language, and interdependence solidifies the argument that these were not two entirely separate cultures but two variations of one common identity within what we now know to be a single, united bioregion. Second, I argue that the area identified by Colin Woodard as "the far west" and identified by Joel Garreau as "the empty quarter," centered on the Rocky Mountains, is only held together as one coherent area today due to the influence of federal control of land. In these two maps, eastern British Columbia, eastern Washington, and eastern Oregon are united in the same region as parts of Manitoba, the Dakotas, and Nebraska. Anti-federalism, or right-of-center libertarian political ideology, does have a relatively large amount of influence in these areas, compared to the rest of the United States and Canada. This could be used as an argument to justify the unity of this large area of the continent, but the prominence of that political philosophy in this area is dependent on the influence of the federal government. Without it, the prominence of this political philosophy dissipates; it is circumstantial and ephemeral, not inherent to this area. Without the influence of our current federal governments, this large area centered upon the Rocky Mountains becomes incoherent and, therefore, more an area of transition between regional cultures than a distinct region upon itself.

In our bioregion of Cascadia, one could travel from Portland, Oregon, to Vancouver, British Columbia, and notice the vast amount of similarity in culture, behavior, economy, and value systems on a societal or a macro level. Even though these two areas are in different ecoregions, they are part of the same philosophical and geographic foundation for societal identity because the ecoregions in which they exist are so similar to one another. The exact demographic makeup of these metropolitan areas may vary, but the shared intangibles within each and between each are undeniable. Both cities exist in a serene landscape that creates a reverence for nature; both cities' economies invest heavily in renewable energy and sustainable technology; and both cities cultivate a tradition of respect for minority identities and lifestyles. I argue the same holds true if one were to travel from Portland, Oregon, to Boise, Idaho. The predominant political persuasions may differ, especially when viewed in a federal prism, but the similarities in culture, behavior, economy, and value systems cannot be ignored or cast away as pure coincidence. For example, even though Portland is a city that often votes heavily in favor of the Democratic Party when it comes to federal politics, and Boise does not, both cities have a countless amount of natural features nearby, used for personal excursion/ recreation. Both cities uphold a strong civil religion of conservation, and both cities' modern economies feature a strong, innovative technology scene. Different localities within a bioregion will have their own distinguishing characteristics that make them unique. Simultaneously, these areas will be compatible with each other, culturally, economically, and otherwise, due to shared environment.

If one was to travel to an area outside of Cascadia, significant and fundamental differences in these intangible entities would be observed. How well a Cascadian could relate to these differences would likely depend on how similar the environment of the bioregion in question is. An individual's personal history, such as if he or she is well traveled, will, of course, also play a role in how well someone can relate to a different area. For example, the American South, which resides in the bioregion of Dixon, has a very different environment, in all that it entails, when compared to Cascadia. The differences in culture, behavior, economy, and value systems between a Cascadian city like Portland, Oregon, and a Dixon city like Birmingham, Alabama, are stark and undeniable. While both cities reside in the same country, the differences in these intangibles are fundamental and, ultimately, irreconcilable in the context of making them similar between these two areas because of their bioregions, which foster them.

These differences can be noticed even in bioregions closer to Cascadia, with some similarities in environments. If one were to travel from Portland, Oregon, to Denver, Colorado—cities both in the American West and surrounded by more rugged, mountainous terrain—there would no doubt be some similarities on a societal level due to some comparable ecoregional elements. However, fundamental differences are observed when one begins to look the basis for culture, behavior, economy, and value systems in these two cities, their surrounding areas, and the bioregions in which they belong. We can better understand this using the economic cluster model for understanding workplace spirituality, as covered in the previous chapter. Both areas have magnificent natural surroundings that are admired and enjoyed by the individuals who live there, which provide for similar expressions of individualism and utilizing nature. However, the Denver area's environment encourages the planning cluster to thrive and more-rigid social and business structures to be maintained, relative to Cascadia. Organized religion in the Denver area is a perfect example of this. While a majority of Portland-area residents do not belong to a church or actively attend organized worship services,[36] a majority of Denver-area residents do.[37] It's difficult to pinpoint these differences and turn this into an exact science, but the ethos felt, experienced, and embodied by individuals within each bioregion is both distinguished and defined at this level. Bioregions are the defining entities of societal ethos, each fostering a distinct sense of identity for the communities that reside in it.

In Cascadia, we experience our lives in the same surroundings; our practices, expressions, and observations of all that encompass our lives—values, beliefs, politics, duties, daily routines, etc.—are affected by those congruent surroundings. Unlike the actuality of our current federal entities, differences between peoples within our bioregional level are not fundamental; they're circumstantial.

We should address two common misconceptions that lead some to initially doubt this theory of bioregionalism in Cascadia. Proving these misconceptions to be false is a key point to embracing the foundation that allows bioregionalism to stand on its own. The first is the belief that cities and towns in Canada (e.g., Kelowna, Vancouver, Victoria) are too different culturally from cities and towns in the United States (e.g., Portland, Seattle, Spokane) and therefore cannot be part of one coherent region. The second is the belief that cities and towns west of the Cascade Mountains (e.g., Portland, Seattle, Vancouver) are too different culturally from cities and towns east of the Cascade Mountains (e.g., Boise, Kelowna, Spokane) and therefore cannot be part of one coherent region. Some who buy into one or both of these notions tend to refer to the dominant political leanings in these given areas, or the differences in population density when comparing urban areas to rural areas, or the differences in the demographic makeup of these given areas. The underlying belief behind these misconceptions is that all within a regionally cohesive culture zone—all who share the same nationhood—should follow the same political leanings, have the same cultural backgrounds, and think in the same way. This belief is inherently flawed due to the realities of human nature. No one nation, if it is to be truly free, will ever unify its people under a single political ideology, force its people to look the same way, or curb everyone's thought processes to follow the same patterns. These are not the things that make a nation. The fact that Spokane votes for the Republican Party at a higher rate than Seattle is irrelevant in this regard. The fact that Vancouver's suburbs have a higher percentage of citizens with Asian ancestry than Boise's suburbs is also irrelevant in this regard. The fact that the Portland area has a stronger urban influence than Yakima is also irrelevant in this regard. The relevant concepts in this regard are the common environment we inherently share and the common guiding principles to our ways of life. This is why we, as a regional collective entity, are capable of uniting and compromising on this level to overcome any problem that faces us.

The question remaining, then, is how, exactly, does a bioregion determine the ethos of a society? Are the environmental aspects the ultimate determining factor in how culture, behavior, economy, and value systems are shaped? Does a bioregion set limits on how these intangibles are practiced and sustained over the course of history rather than ultimately determine them? Or does a bioregion simply set a unique foundation for these intangibles, which allows them to be differentiated across the continent while allowing the human condition and free will to set limits? There is not one clear answer agreed upon by those who have studied this concept. I am inclined to believe, however, that a bioregion uses its environmental makeup to set boundaries (both physical and metaphorical) on the practices of these intangible elements of society while we, as human beings with free will, determine how these intangibles are expressed. In other words, bioregions do not determine our actions or solidify our fate as a society; free will determines those.

But bioregions do set limits on our actions, interactions, and our practices as communities, directing them to conform to the ethos sustainable to its environment. We can refer to the experiences of the immigrants who arrived to Cascadia more than one hundred years ago to exemplify this hypothesis:

> On September 4, 1906, Arthur Van Ackere, a Belgian immigrant farmer recently arrived in Oregon's Tualatin Valley, wrote to his brother-in-law, Emil Duyck, who was working as a coachman in Rock Island, Illinois, "The Belgians around here don't get along too well." Three decades of letters among this extended immigrant family contain repeated comment on how, in Oregon, the Belgians do not co-operate with each other as they did in Illinois or Iowa ... While none of the letter writers offers an explanation for why, the persistence of the theme and repeated comparison with the Belgian community in the Midwest suggest that the issues involved more than clashing personalities. Something happened to the Belgians in this new place. What happened to them occurred in other immigrant ethnic communities and among other in-migrants to the region who referred to themselves simply as "Americans" or "Canadians" as well. What happened to these immigrants continues to occur. People who enter Cascadia experience a loosening of connection to social institutions that may be experienced as exhilarating, frightening, or both. At the same time, they experience a natural geography of scale

and grandeur. What results in Cascadia, where social and geographic landscapes are intertwined, is a rethinking of identity and community.[38]

What worked in another region of the country did not work in Cascadia; the influence of the environment and the ways of living it produces changed the cultural norms of those who immigrated there.

This phenomenon experienced by Arthur Van Ackere continues today, as the bioregion of Cascadia itself molds the communities within it. For example, the mountainous terrain around the Puget Sound prevents the greater Seattle area from becoming too densely populated. The society at large could choose to expand population centers in neighboring areas that are harder to reach and maintain, but the impracticality of this prospect prevents such a thing from happening. Hence, the environment sets limitations on and influences city planning in the Puget Sound area. Another example can be how the natural resources in that area help determine its economy. An entrepreneur could import a significant amount of non-native resources to try to capitalize on a certain market, but the expense and instability of this prospect prevents such a practice from becoming prominent. This is why no sugar cane or citrus farms exist in Cascadia; the region's environment doesn't support the natural cultivation of these resources. Attempting to begin such a farm in the region would be extremely costly and would most likely result in heavily lost profits. Another example can be how the surrounding areas, ripe with lesser-developed land

and temperate ecosystems, provide prime opportunities for persons to enjoy outdoor activities. A social organization meant to bring structure, order, and interconnectivity to a large area could grow in popularity and expand its influence, but the opportunities for excursion, exploration, reflection, and enjoyment by individuals limit the prospects of any one organization's expanding its sphere of influence to dominate any competition. This region does not set society's fate or the fate of any individual, but it does set limits on practices that are able to thrive and, over time, filter the actions and interactions of society at large to conform with the ethos of this region.

On this same note, this phenomenon results in similar trends developing throughout the entirety of the population within a bioregion. This ensures that even across local diversities, the intangibles that in our case make Cascadia "Cascadian," in terms of identity, are able to be unified across the entire region. Our interdependence is intrinsic—an action made by an individual or a group of individuals regarding the environment or the economy affects others within our bioregion inherently more-so than others outside of it. The effects from our interdependence, rooted in our bioregional foundation, encourage us to be compatible. This provides an explanation to why and how our ethos is maintained after shifts in population size, demographics, or cultural backgrounds. In the previous chapter, I proposed that the ethos of the Cascadian region was composed in the same manner before and after European settlement. If we understand bioregions as limits on the societal components of ethos, it would explain why the ethos was maintained over hundreds of years and massive population changes. The makeup of a bioregional ethos is sustained even though the specifics of how this ethos is expressed changes with the course of human events. This holds true in the age of globalization, where levels of shared information and experiences are at unprecedented highs. Take Cascadia's relation to other regions in the United States or Canada as an example. The outward identity of the Cascadian region has shifted massively over the past two hundred years. Settlers from regions such as New England or the Mid-Atlantic/Midwest settled in large numbers, completely shifting the demographic makeup of the region. Furthermore, they introduced practices and traditions not native to the Cascadian region. It's true that the differences between the distinctions of Cascadia and these other regions, culturally or otherwise, dissipated with time and movement of people between these regions, thereby exposing the traditions once held in one place and being brought to another, but the macro-level ethos of Cascadia continued to be based upon its environment because of the unique limitations it sets. Therefore, the ethos between Cascadia and any other bioregion will always be fundamentally different in some way, as long as the Cascadian environment remains unique and distinguished as such, even though these ethos (plural) fluctuate and possibly become less differentiated with an increase in shared culture over time. Practices for tradition's sake eventually will dissolve. But practices that survive because they are optimal for the region, maintaining a relevant purpose, will remain.

In the context of our present time, the social movement to recognize and reclaim Cascadia's regional identity in this sense has already begun. We have the potential to begin a new narrative as the united region of Cascadia, which embraces our possibilities and maximizes the potential within our own region. Such a reality will not be realized through drastic means of force but through the natural evolution of our thoughts—a gradual awakening of societal consciousness. The values that help construct the Cascadian narrative—our ethos and our ways of life—exist in our public consciousness already and conflict with the dominant, imperialist narratives of Canada and the United States. This is the biggest reason, at the most basic level, why our current federal systems of governance and cooperation are not functioning properly. Our distinct environments have created distinct identities that have emerged stronger with time and population growth. As our federal organizations and political parties focus on fewer and fewer areas of ideology, which remain relatively unified across just a few affiliated groups, our differences as regions within our two countries become stark. And as long as we look to the current systems in place for a solution— an answer that will unite either country in one common ethos—we will be left frustrated and bewildered. Just as people cannot move mountains, people cannot resolve the fundamental differences between societies that are instilled by nature in order to make them identical. If we are to make progress on any of these issues that plague us, however, these regional (read: national) differences must be recognized and addressed as they are and not simply as we wish to see them.

The answer we seek is through bioregionalism; it explains why our political systems are so dysfunctional now and gives us direction towards the next step in evolving that reality for Cascadia. Any system that truly allows bioregionalism to thrive will have two fundamentally different components that will help us steer away from the imperialist nature the United States and Canada embraced after their original establishments. First, it will ensure that the state,[iii] which creates laws to govern its citizens and interacts as a single entity with other states, is formed around a coherent and congruent foundation for societal culture and identity; a bioregional ethos is common while the variances between its local diversities and its ecoregions are minimal. To expand political borders past bioregional barriers as determined by geography would be to dominate communities with a fundamentally different natural environment and ethos. Forcing such communities to abide by laws influenced from the dominant natural ethos that is not their own, or co-opting their natural resources not indigenous to the dominant bioregion, is imperialist and inherently corruptive. Second, it will create a legal foundation that recognizes the inherent rights of all living communities, taking human beings off an ivory tower of relative infallibility and acknowledging the inalienable and tangible rights of nature. These natural surroundings and living

---

iii   "State" refers to an autonomous political entity on an international level (i.e., a country).

systems are what make bioregional nationhood possible. Destroying or attempting to utterly deplete these natural elements of society is to assume humankind is above nature and above the force that created it. To affirm such a philosophy creates an unsustainable condition for society to exist in peace and interdependence.

We can pave a new path, realizing our nationhood with our environment and naturally influenced ethos. We can be the New Age example that turns away from ethnocentricity and affirms that nationhood based on ancient tribalism and ethnic exclusivity is nothing more than an archaic philosophy that limits possibility. We can look past the surface-level social divisions imposed on us by our current federal political systems. We should not be separated by liberal and conservative worldviews, political party affiliation, urban and rural settings, ethnic and racial differences, disparities in our personal wealth, or, most certainly, the arbitrary international borders as they exist today. We do not have to choose between our local differences east and west of the Cascade Mountain Range in an attempt to gain a dominant influence throughout the entire region; we're in this together as Cascadians, regardless of our differences, whatever they may be. We can accomplish fundamental political change peacefully, should we choose to pursue it, using debate and the democratic processes afforded us by our constitutional principles in the United States and Canada. And in order to do this effectively, we need to be able to turn a political argument over identity, borders, and resources into a human argument about what it means to be free.

4. FREEDOM AS BALANCE

Who are we as a people? What is our purpose? These questions don't have definitive, irrefutable answers, but they have crossed our minds at one time or another. They've crossed the minds of civilizations for as long as humans have had the level of sentience to ponder them. Stories have been told for generations in many civilizations on the planet about their respective origins, their history, their traditions, and their driving aspirations. Stories of past events are recorded and studied in order to gain understanding. Stories of religious significance have united entire societies in purpose and action. Human beings have attempted to answer these and other similar questions through the medium of narrative. That's how we form our sense of understanding the world in which we live and how we make sense of everything in our lives, seen and unseen, making stories very powerful tools. Human beings are, essentially, storytellers; we process and analyze the world around us in the narrative form. Our intangible surroundings, which provide meaning, are full of competing stories from which we choose in a continual process of adaptation and re-creation. We choose them, thereby achieving a sense of understanding, based on their coherence and fidelity—whether or not they hold together as plausible and fit with our value systems or preexisting understanding. Our decision-making process—our rationality—is based on the understanding acquired from these stories.[39] This paradigm of the human condition—the narrative paradigm—was introduced just three decades ago by Walter Fisher, professor emeritus of the Annenberg School of Communication at the University of Southern California. It explains that human beings are not, as previously understood, logical animals that analyze the world in the form of logical puzzles solved by evidential reasoning and discussion. One need take only a few moments to research the technicalities within the formal study of logic to conclude that we, as human beings, most certainly do not analyze and understand the world in such a fashion on an everyday basis. We use our own experiences, take stories we've heard that have provided meaning to us, and fit them together in a way that makes sense to achieve further meaning and purpose. We keep the stories that fit our values and our rationality in order to continue learning and adapting as human beings, whereas we reject the stories that aren't compatible with these components of our awareness.

One prominent question human beings have attempted to answer is this: what is freedom? Or what does it mean to be free? In Canada and especially the United States, our understanding of what it means to be free in America comes, in part, from the story of the American dream. The narrative of freedom via financial prosperity and wealth has been a part of the North American story for the better part of the past 150 years—being able to start a new life, unhindered from authority, work hard, and, with a little luck, be wildly successful to achieve fame and fortune. It's a story that tells all people, regardless of who they are or what their background is, that they can work hard and become economically prosperous on this continent. This narrative of the American dream has set the framework for what it means to be free. It's a mythical reality—something that almost everyone believes he or she can do but something that is actually achieved, in all the narrative entails in the romantic sense, by very few. That does not mean the story and its motives are without merit; certainly we want to be able to live our lives without the burden of oppression, be able to work hard and live honestly, and be able to enjoy a comfortable life as a result. But what has happened is that this narrative has been twisted over time to equate freedom with money, consumption, and a lack of collective values. It's a narrative that falsely assumes that resources are unlimited, not finite to our planet, and that exploiting them will have no lasting effect on society. It's a narrative that says freedom is realized through wealth, and any collective action to alter an individual's wealth is therefore wrong. And perhaps most dangerously, it's a narrative that has evolved, in some areas, to conclude that freedom is absolutely based in the individual and that there's only one way to achieve it: through economic domination.

Both of our current countries, forged in the era of expansion through colonialism, are predicated on a narrative of liberty through dominance and ownership of land, possessions, and monetary value. In the United States

and Canada, these things often determine our perceptions of freedom; they help form our understanding of
it. Our politics, value systems, culture, laws, and economy
are based on these perceptions—the ones that say freedom is realized through our ability to purchase goods; or
our ability to utilize purchased land for whatever purpose
we desire; or when no legitimized public body is able to
curb individual behavior of consumption. However, this
narrative and these perceptions, unto themselves, are
based on another story.[i][40] The narrative that attempts to
answer the question of what it means to be free and that
is the foundation for the American dream can best be
titled the "story of the self." This story says that you are an
autonomous and independent individual, fundamentally
disconnected from the world around you.[41] It says that
you are separate from other individuals and that you exist in a universe that is separate from you.[42] Extrapolating
this story to understand what freedom means creates a
basis centered on individuality. To be free means that you
are able to act optimally as an individual, independent
from others and the world in which you live. Anything
that acts as an obstacle to this notion is, therefore, contrary to freedom. This story also explicitly implies that
actions made by other individuals, or the events that
occur in the lives of other people, do not matter unless

---

i   In December 2012, filmmakers associated with the group
Cascadia Matters released a documentary, *Occupied Cascadia*,
which has an introduction that summarizes this premise. The
following paragraphs paraphrase and expand upon this introduction.

they directly affect you in the present. In this sense, any actions you make that have a direct negative impact on another individual constitutes a violation of that person's freedom. Likewise, any negative action by another person unto you is a violation of your freedom. It is from this rationality that common law prohibiting certain actions (e.g., assault) can be agreed upon by a collective group in order to protect the freedom of all. But other than that, freedom is solely individual.

It's from this rationality that we justify the objectification of natural living communities as resources purely for human consumption. Human beings see the world as a material thing to be utilized for their needs and desires alike.[43] According to this story of the self, the autonomous individual has domain over what he or she can acquire. Stone, trees, water, plants, and animals are subject to what he or she wishes to do with them; any suggestion otherwise would be a limitation of individual autonomy and therefore an unjustified limitation on freedom. After all, as long as this individual does not use these resources to directly harm anyone else, what moral right does anyone else have to coerce this individual into using these resources in any other way than the manner he or she sees fit?

This story of the self makes sense to us to some extent; it holds together with narrative coherence and is, therefore, plausible. It also has validity, or narrative fidelity, with our value systems and our experiences as human beings. If we, as a people, did not find this narrative rational, it would not have been passed down and adapted by generation after generation. However, it's a relatively new story that has only gained prominence in Western civilization since the eighteenth century.

Opposite this narrative is a much older, more prominent story called the "story of the whole." This story says that the community, or the society at large, is the autonomous and independent entity, in which all who reside in it work and live in an optimal way for the purpose of ensuring the collective entity's survival and preservation. The "whole"—the sum of the individuals who make up this society—is personified as an individual. The understanding of freedom from this narrative is that no such thing as individual liberty exists, at least not in the way we're used to thinking of individual liberty via the story of the self. This story presumes that in order for all to thrive, all must embrace the one true way of living life righteously. If everyone knows this and what is required in order to achieve this goal, everyone will gladly accept "the system" in accordance. But in reality, not everyone is "enlightened" enough to buy into such a system. It is the duty of those with the most knowledge—who, by the rationality attained from the belief that there exists only one attainable truth, must all be in agreement in the conclusions surmised from this knowledge—to lead and enlighten the rest of society. Individual liberty is only realized when one gains this knowledge, reaches the same conclusions, and becomes enlightened.

In this story, there is no such thing as an individual's right to be wrong; this is not individual liberty but despotism that enslaves the individual in ignorance. Rights and privileges are granted to individuals from designated authorities within that society, but inherent liberty, as we're used to thinking of liberty in the United States and Canada, belongs only to the society as whole. And in order for the "whole" to be free from exterior forces that may coerce or oppress it, it usually requires much work and sacrifice from the individuals within it. The greater good comes first, while the needs and desires of individuals come second. This narrative can be traced back to Plato, who spoke of philosopher kings ruling over society in his version of utopia.[ii] It has been used to justify the authority of monarchies and dictatorships throughout the ages. However, it has also been used to justify the importance of community and realizing our inherent dependency on one another as individuals in order to thrive. I could argue that this story of the whole serves as the basis for the popular or most common interpretations of much of the teachings given by Jesus of Nazareth, who fiercely advocated for fellowship and selflessly giving away what you have—be they material goods, food, wealth, or talents—to others in need. It's the story that affirms no individual is infallible, and no one's individual desires are above the needs of the many.

Both the story of the self and the story of the whole have been used to answer the unanswerable and, thus, give us an understanding of what freedom is. However, these diametrically opposing narratives aren't the only two that seek to give us a basis for understanding. There

---

ii   See Plato's *Republic.*

is another story—one that says you are an autonomous individual *not* disconnected from the world around you. This story says that an individual is the totality of the relationships she or he has; that his or her actions and interactions with others matter.[44] It is also a story that says you live in a world where everyone is fundamentally connected to one another. It provides an explanation to why you feel a sense of joy and justice when you see a story on the evening news about someone overcoming adversity to achieve something great, or when you feel a sense of sorrow and pain when you see children, half a world away, suffering from famine. This story has been referred to as the "story of the people," but I believe this title gives a subtle connotation of opposition to the story of the self. Therefore, I believe a more apt title for this story is the "story of the connected self"—a story where the individual and the community are meant to coexist with one another. When extrapolating upon this story to understand what freedom means, it creates a basis centered on balance. To be free means not only to be able to have control over your own actions and your own will but also to be able to come together as a community to ensure that the same liberties and opportunities are afforded to all and prohibited by none. The notion of individual actions having a direct effect on other individuals, constituting a violation of their freedom, still exists under this narrative. However, it does not neglect the indirect effects your decisions have on other individuals, nor does it neglect the decisions of other individuals made upon other individuals.

Nor, with the understanding of one being connected to the world in which one lives, does it neglect the actions of individuals made upon the living communities that surround them—animal life, plant life, and the natural environment. An individual shares in the successes and failures of others, be it tangibly or emotionally. To be free, as an individual and as a community, is to actualize this. Freedom is realized not exclusively as individual or collective but as a dichotomy in which the individual and communal aspects exist together as one.

This is the story upon which Cascadia's understanding of freedom is—and should be—based. It's why we, as individuals in this region, fiercely advocate for individuals' right to self-expression and living as they choose, while simultaneously we are fiercely protective of our environment and revere our natural surroundings. It is through the story of the connected self that we acquire the sense of rationality that explains how our cherished sense of individuality is supposed to work with our communities and our surrounding environment. Whether we consciously realize this or not, Cascadia is the region in which the story of the connected self is dominant. We're beginning to realize that the American dream, as it is known, is not the full story, nor is it the Cascadian story. To Cascadians across the entire political spectrum, the American dream has been perverted in recent decades and has come into direct and irreconcilable conflict with Cascadia's identity. Freedom here is not achieved by economically dominating everything else that one deems inferior or through consumption and authority of the economic elite. Freedom is a balance, a two-way street between individualism and collectivism.

We are living through the effects of other regions having instilled their identity and their values, based on the desire for maximum individual autonomy, in our federal systems of governance, which collide with our regional reality. Our federal identities have been altered by this false narrative of domination that tells us what it means to be free. As a consequence, these American and Canadian identities have become contrary to our Cascadian identity—not the exact opposite per se but certainly no longer compatible. This does not mean we oppose these contradictions with hostility, but it does mean we need to accept that our legitimacy to function as united federal systems has been broken. It also means that our freedom as Cascadians and as a single region of Cascadia is diminished as we're being coerced by institutionalism, both public and private, to live in a manner not optimal for our own society. The dominance of the story of the self perpetuates into Cascadia via this institutionalism, which results in our environment and our livelihoods being threatened[iii] as we, having public institutions (e.g., town/city councils, state/provincial legislatures, regional business, nonprofit organizations) that are unable to unite and/or inadequate to stand up for our interests as one people, are incapable of stopping this coercion, regardless of how many of us wish to. The story of the self

iii   Oil pipeline construction in British Columbia, coal depot/ train route proposals in Idaho, Oregon, and Washington, fracking proposals in Oregon and Northern California, etc.

can no longer be the basis for rationalizing freedom in Cascadia, lest we succumb to the inevitable and outright subjugation to this institutionalism that originates from outside Cascadia's mountainous borders.

Before I go any further, I am obligated to clarify the distinction between the notion of liberty and the notion of freedom. In the United States and Canada, we often use these terms interchangeably, as do even some of the most brilliant contemporary political philosophers. I, however, assert that these two concepts are not equal to one another. Furthermore, I assert that it is essential to the notion of freedom as balance that these two concepts be fundamentally different, albeit strongly related, entities. "Liberty" comes from the ancient Greek and Roman concept of *libertas*—a notion of civil privilege granted to the elite in society.[45] Only those privileged enough were able to act relatively free from the coercion of others and exercise decision-making power. While we now reject the severe exclusivity it once took to obtain and exercise basic civil liberty, the concept of liberty is and should be understood as a subject pertaining to action—being able to act towards one's will, free from the coercion of others. "Freedom" comes from the Western European concept of *freiheit*—a notion that all people (or all men, as was understood at the time) were born free and all should be treated equally under civil law.[46] According to this concept, all are born with liberty, and all should be able to act according to individual will. Thus, the concept of freedom should be understood as a subject pertaining to possession—having liberty in order to act towards one's will, free from the coercion of others. To summarize, you are free if you have liberty, and you have liberty if you are able to act towards your own will. And while it is true that to be free means you are able to act towards your own will, it is liberty that allows you to take such actions; freedom is simply the status of having or living with liberties. The liberties and freedom I will focus on in this book are those pertaining to civil and/or political means; that is, the concepts of freedom and liberty relevant to the discussion I'm perpetuating pertain to the civil and/or political sphere of influence, rather than the physical, spiritual, or other existential spheres of influence. So when I refer to liberty as being able to act towards one's will, any obstacles that would prevent such liberty from being exercised would come from other people and not an inability to do so from one's own being.[47] Furthermore, the liberties I will elaborate on should be understood on both the individual and collective levels. I assert that each has liberties relative to the other. The individual has liberty to act within society, while simultaneously, the collective (e.g., the state, or the government), whose decision-making power is executed as a single entity, even though it's composed of multiple people, also has liberty to act within that society, with respect to the individuals within it. Understanding and acknowledging these distinctions—the difference between liberty and freedom, the concept of political liberties and freedom, and the concept of individual and collective liberties with respect to one another—is vital to understanding the arguments made in this book.

All three stories—the story of the self, the story of the whole, and the story of the connected self—have narrative coherence and fidelity. All three stories attempt to answer the questions pertaining to our nature and our existence. In doing so, they provide a foundation for us to base rationalization off of. Two of these stories—of the self and of the whole—are absolute; they create a basis for meaning that exists in only one aspect: either with the individual or with the collective. Any attempt to apply the rationality derived from one of these narrative frameworks to the reality of the aspect opposite causes the framework to break and the narrative, thus all rationality and understanding that stems from it, to be rendered moot. For example, when extrapolating from the story of the self to understand the concept of freedom, the rationality derived from that narrative cannot be adapted for a purpose that does not form to the same foundation. Society couldn't pass a law to limit individual autonomy pertaining to a condition outside the parameters of ensuring that any one individual cannot cause direct harm to another; such a collective decision would constitute a violation of individual autonomy and, thus, be determined as contrary to freedom. Likewise, the rationality derived from the story of the whole cannot be adapted to support the notion that individuals should be allowed to live in a manner they see fit for themselves, if such a manner counters the expectations set forth to optimize society for a collective purpose. Should an individual choose to act contrary to the will of the whole, it would jeopardize faith in the system that is meant for the greater good and, thus, be seen as contrary to freedom. These models of rationality do not ignore that the opposite aspect exists, but each has an absolute framework that holds up only if all understanding that comes from it operates in only one aspect. The other story, the connected self, is fluctuant and conditional. It creates a basis for meaning that exists in both aspects and *cannot* be limited to one or the other. The rationality derived from this narrative framework demands that a balance exist between individuality and community in order for freedom to be attained. Should the equilibrium skew in favor of one aspect over the other, then individual or collective liberty (whichever aspect is being undermined) diminishes and forces of control become dominant, thus violating the notion of freedom. Both aspects must be recognized as two inseparable halves—two opposite forces working together as one entity.

According to the story of the self—the primary story that serves as the foundation for understanding liberty and freedom in the United States and Canada—any sort of collective rule to curb behavior or prevent certain actions, lest direct harm be done to another, is irrational. This, in theory, seems like a reasonable foundation for civil law in our society. I claim that this foundation is necessary, in part, for a free society to exist. But if we use this story and its absolutist nature on its own to understand what freedom means practically and how it's protected when threatened, we are forced to accept a level of individualism that I believe most in Cascadia would find unacceptable. Let's say you are a wealthy entrepreneur, and you have your sights set on some land, on which you want to build a factory. The factory is built and is capable of producing the volume of products you need to sell to maintain profitability, but there are some concerns. First, in producing the goods you intend to sell, the factory produces hazardous waste. The best option, from a pure cost-benefit point of view, is to dump this waste in the river next to the factory. No towns nearby use the river as a source of drinking water or for any other purpose similar, so you wouldn't be in danger of poisoning other people directly. According to the rationality of the story of the self, it should be completely in your right to dump this waste in the river. It may have some negative effect on wildlife and plants, but these are commodities that shouldn't have an effect on your rights as an autonomous individual. If the municipality in which the factory is located were to levy a law that prevents you from dumping this hazardous waste into the river, this law would be a direct violation of your liberties. As such, this law would not exist in a society that understands liberty and freedom, according to the story of the self. The individual is the sole benefactor of liberty, according to this story, and this decision made by a collective entity would be completely irrational and unjust.

Let's take this example one step further. The undeveloped land on which you want to build this factory is owned by somebody who does not wish to develop this land for any purpose. You've analyzed many practical possibilities, and this piece of land is most optimal for your chances at maximum profitability. You decide you're going to buy this land from the current owner. You're even going to pay more than the land is worth because you're confident you'll win big in the long term. You make an offer, and the current owner decides he or she doesn't want to sell at any price. This person is now an obstacle to your acting according to your own will and is coercing you to make another decision, one you would otherwise not make. According to the story of the self, this is a violation of your freedom as an autonomous individual and, theoretically, it should be within your rights to overcome this obstacle to attain what you wish, as long as you don't cause direct harm to this other individual. You decide to go ahead and start building the factory anyway, even though you don't own the land. You have more resources, more money, and more power than this other individual, and the only way he can stop you alone is to cause you direct harm. After all, in a society in which freedom is solely an entity belonging to the individual, any law that says you shouldn't be able to use this land however you see fit is irrational.

Obviously, these examples present a paradox. How can freedom be maintained in such a society if your decisions coerce others to make decisions they would otherwise not make? For example, what if someone wanted to swim in the river in which you dump your waste but cannot because it could endanger his or her health? Does your decision to dump waste into the river constitute a violation of that person's freedom, according to the story of the self? Yet if that person used any authority authorized by a collective (i.e., a government entity) to stop you from dumping waste into the river, it would be a violation of your freedom, according to the story of the self. What of the owner whose land you just forcibly took? Doesn't your decision coerce that person, as an autonomous individual, against his or her will? That should be considered a violation of his or her freedom, according to the story of the self. Yet any law to prevent you from taking this land is unjust if the story of the self is to be the sole foundation for freedom and liberty in society. If the story of the self is the only foundation for understanding what liberty and freedom are, then conflict is inevitable. And the only way to absolutely secure your freedom, when the liberties of individuals clash, is for you, as an individual, to dominate what is inferior. If others really wanted to stop you from dumping hazardous waste, building this factory, or developing land you do not own, their only course of action is to try to dominate you, thereby removing the obstacle to their freedom. Causing direct harm to another may be appropriately against the law in this society, but self-defense and protecting your liberties as an individual would be perfectly rational and justified. Taking up arms against you would be considered self-defense for them, as they would be acting to protect their liberties. Your using physical force in retaliation of their attack would be considered self-defense, as you would be acting to protect your liberties. The end result would be one party in this conflict being dominated and/or eliminated entirely.

It is clear to me that this formula for society—this impossibly individualistic rationality, which comes from the same foundational story that serves as the basis for how most in the United States and Canada currently understand freedom and liberty—should not be the pinnacle we strive to reach as human beings or as a united nation of people.

Likewise, according to the story of the whole, any allowance for individuals to act in manner contrary to or outside the parameters of the expectations set forth by society at large, whether or not it's a democratic majority, is irrational. The rights of a governing body to pass laws can surely be considered legitimate. Both the United States and Canada have federal legislatures, state/provincial legislatures, and town/city councils that have the responsibility and obligation to pass laws, but giving absolute liberty to any collective entity would provide for a reality just as conflicting and paradox-ridden as the one that operates according to the story of the self. The arguments against this foundational story of the whole should be self-evident in cases of autocratic societies or dictatorships, in which the citizenry have no rights to influence the laws or organizations that govern them. For the sake of argument, let's assume we're referring to democratic societies in which there are no autonomous rulers or dictators with supreme power. The governing bodies of such societies are directly elected by the people and are charged with making laws in order to govern. To start off with a rather extreme example that would require severe government intrusion to enforce, let's say a municipality within such a society passes a law forbidding the eating of fruit on Wednesdays; there's a shortage of fresh fruit, and the democratically-elected legislature for this municipality passed this law in an attempt to curb consumption. If any individual disobeyed this rule by consuming an apple on a Wednesday evening, thus violating the expectations set forth by a democratically elected government, he or she would be undermining the collective system and violating the freedom of that community as a result. According to the story of the whole, in which society at large is only free if all those within it embrace the expectations set forth by the governing body, an individual does not have the right to disobey a law, regardless of whether she or he deems it irrational. Such a judgment is not up to individuals to make, and any individual in violation of any such law, regardless of the circumstance, must be punished. For if any one individual deems a law to be irrational and defies it or argues for its defiance, the freedom of the collective as a whole is put at risk. The individual, in this case, must be deemed irrational if she or he disagrees with the reasoning behind this law and must be coerced out of her or his false worldview.

Let's use another, more applicable example to today's status quo. Let's say a society has a standing law offering civil privileges and tax benefits to couples who have committed to living their lives together, but only couples composed of one man and one woman may enter into this civil contract, according to the laws passed by the democratically elected governing body. The democratic majority has decided that the coupling of one man and one woman is ideal to ensure the survival and perpetuation of their society and has thus made such civil contracts exclusive to opposite-sex coupling. If a man in this society wanted to commit to living with another man, that desire, as well as his desire for his relationship to be viewed as equal under the law, is irrelevant. His sexual orientation—an intrinsic characteristic to his very being—is also irrelevant. According to the story of the whole, this individual has no grounds for his will to be expressed in this scenario. Any attempt to defy the expectations set out by the collective is thereby irrational and subversive—a threat to the freedom of that society. An act as simple as expressing opposition to such a law, thereby refuting the rationale of the collective, is worthy of punishment.

In these scenarios, the only way for society to ensure its freedom survives is by duly punishing the individuals who have not only broken the law but merely deem the law to be wrong. Freedom is secured by allowing the collective whole to dominate the inferior individual by forcing punishment against his or her will. Only then can order be restored, and society can resume its course undisturbed by those who wish to defy it. The rationality for such power to be wielded by the collective comes with the assumption that there is, or at least should be, one "correct" way to live in a given society. In these scenarios, the democratic majorities have the right to create laws sanctioning the behavior the collective believes to be right. Individuals within this society do not have the liberty to be wrong. The ultimate ends of what is deemed to be objectively true must coincide with the beliefs and actions of the people within this society, no matter how strongly one may object to compliance.[48] There is no such thing as freedom to be wrong or irrational. Forcing compliance is not an act of tyranny but an act of compassion that will allow any such individual to be liberated from his or her bondage of irrationality.[49] Freedom is not the ability to follow your own will as an autonomous individual but to understand and accept the rules of society. When individuals gain necessary knowledge and understand this, they will be preserved from the aggravation that comes from attempting that which is impossible, according to society's rationale.[50]

The underlying assumption of this rationality is that the knowledge procured and acted upon by the collective must be true, and laws made to govern society in accordance with this truth must therefore be right. Here's where the paradox comes into play: what if, in the universal or objective sense, the majority is wrong? What if the knowledge procured by the collective in order to make these laws was incorrect, or incomplete, or insufficient in some other manner? Surely no individual or group of individuals is infallible. Therefore, the possibility must exist that the individuals who make up the collective might be wrong. If the individuals in the previous scenarios who argued against the laws of society were actually right, in an objective sense, and the laws imposed upon the individuals were therefore wrong, then the framework provided by the story of the whole falls apart. Or at least it dictates that the democratic majority is obligated to change the laws of society, even if most do not wish to do so. Obviously, such an outcome is unlikely in a society where majority rules absolutely.

We can even take this paradox one step further: what if no such thing as a universal objective truth exists? Or if it does exist, what if understanding this truth requires an omnipresence that human beings cannot physically attain? Contemporary political philosopher Isaiah Berlin summarizes this point as eloquently as anyone:

> It seems to me that the belief that some single formula can in principle be found whereby all the diverse ends of men can be harmoniously realized is demonstrably false. If, as I believe, the ends of men are many, and not all of them are in principle compatible with each other, then the possibility of conflict—and of tragedy—can never wholly be eliminated from human life, either personal or social. The necessity of choosing between absolute claims is then an inescapable characteristic of the human condition.[51]

Determining what is "right" will always be conditional and relative to the circumstance, and it may differ from individual to individual, depending on the circumstance. The absolute liberties of the collective, according to the story of the whole, are therefore completely irrational because they depend on the collective being universally and objectively correct. This is not to say that governing bodies shouldn't exist, or that every decision made by a collective is wrong but that their liberties to make and execute laws must not be absolute, as they are according to the foundational story of the whole.

Rationality derived purely from the story of the whole, much like the story of the self, is unrealistically and impossibly absolute. Furthermore, securing freedom when it's threatened requires the domination or elimination of the inferior obstacle/individual(s). Again, this is eerily similar to the story of the self, where freedom can only exist in one aspect, according to the rationality derived from the narrative. It is for these reasons I argue the story of the whole should also not be the foundation for understanding or interpreting liberty and freedom. The basis we seek can be found by accepting the practical reality pointed out by Berlin in the previous quote—that the inevitable conflict between absolute claims is inescapable. By accepting this, we acknowledge that freedom cannot exist in just one aspect—individual or collective—at all times. By accepting this, we acknowledge that freedom must exist with the combination of both aspects working simultaneously with and against each other as two inseparable halves. And by acknowledging these truths, we must accept that freedom requires the conditional flexibility to choose, on a micro-level, between individual and collective liberties. To put it another way, we must accept that freedom requires the ability for an individual to acknowledge individual or collective liberty in a given situation, which may mean that society acknowledges one kind of liberty or both simultaneously.

This is the rationality derived from the foundational story of the connected self. Allowing a collective body to instill rules of law outside the strict parameters of direct harm from one individual unto another is just as rational, given the circumstances, as allowing an individual to act according to his or her own will, even if such acts are met with disapproval by the majority of others. Through the connected self, we acknowledge that we are simultaneously autonomous individuals with individual wills and are inherently connected to the community and environment around us. It is essential, therefore, that liberties of both the individual and the collective be recognized as legitimate. In any specific circumstance, should we accept the story of the connected self as the foundation for understanding the concepts of liberty and freedom, we as individuals will choose to affirm the rights of an individual (or group of individuals) and/or affirm the rights of the community. The liberties of both can be legitimate, but the choices made will be done in the interest of ensuring a status quo that is balanced and, therefore, free.

For instance, let's say a democratic majority levies a tax on a community to pay for public schooling. From an individual's point of view, this could be seen as a violation of his liberty because he is being coerced to pay money he would otherwise not pay. Or it could be seen as an affirmation of her liberty because she will now be able to get an education she otherwise could not afford. From the society's point of view, you're accepting the legitimacy of both these absolute claims but choosing to support one, while simultaneously affirming the collective's liberty to take action as a single entity, according to the will of its majority. The end goal of this specific decision is done to ensure the presence of freedom. And because freedom, in its universal and timeless notion, cannot exist absolutely in either the individual or collective aspect, the choice of affirming certain liberties, in this circumstance, is geared towards a macro-level balance of liberties, which results in a status that widely can be considered and acknowledged as "free." If, after considering the totality of circumstances present and instances that occur at any given point in time, the liberties of both the individual and the collective are balanced, the story of the connected self leads to a societal framework of popular sovereignty (the right of the people to govern themselves), mutual dependence (the need for individuals to rely on one another to ensure freedom's existence through both individual and communal means), and egalitarianism (the notion that each individual or living entity is equal to one another in terms of fundamental worth or value). If you subscribe to the rationality that individual and communal liberty both exist, then you must understand freedom in terms of the connected self and discard the narratives of the self and the whole, both of which are mutually exclusive from one another. The absolutist bases for understanding—the story of the self and the story of the whole—leave no room for balance or practical application to reality and *must* be rejected.

In Cascadia, that means we must move past the notion that freedom is predominately an individual entity. The communal aspect of liberty may be opposite of individual liberty, but it is not an opposing force to freedom. Communal liberty, or collective liberty, is an expression of our interdependence as a people, which makes freedom possible. It allows a society of individuals to create a system of cooperation that allows any individual the right to take advantage of opportunity, thereby allowing for an individual to follow his or her intuition and contribute to the growth of society, as well as his or her own well-being. This is how freedom is actualized: the rationality of individual and communal liberty working together as opposite, mutually dependent forces of the same system. Freedom is realized when a society allows individuality to flourish and encourages individuals to unite under their own free will to promote reason and justice. Freedom is not realized when individuals cease their methods of interdependence, a reality of the human condition that cannot simply dissolve because it doesn't coincide with certain individual desires. Nor is it realized when society compels or predetermines individual action without the consent or input of the individual. Communal liberty is both an obligation and a natural component of freedom. Just as we were born to be free as autonomous individuals, part of that freedom is the connection we have with the world around us. *Non nobis solum nati sumus*—not unto ourselves alone are we born.[iv]

Freedom also requires the power to choose and the power to act without unjust obstacles: the liberty to act or not act, according to your own will to an appropriate extent and the liberty to act or not act with minimal

---

iv   This is the motto of my alma mater, Willamette University, and one I've taken to heart.

coercion from others.[v] This is the inherent nature of freedom that coincides with the dichotomy between the power of an individual to choose and act, or not act, and the power of a community to choose and act, or not act. These notions and the difference between them—to be free to choose and to be free from coercion—are established bedrocks of classical liberal philosophy defined and furthered by the writings of John Stuart Mill and Isaiah Berlin—positive liberty and negative liberty.

Positive liberty can best be summarized as having the ability and power to fulfill self-determined potential. To paraphrase a statement of personal application coined by Isaiah Berlin, positive liberty is realized when one can say "I am my own master."[52] Negative liberty is the opposite perspective: to have autonomy over one's own actions without the interference of others. To paraphrase Isaiah Berlin again, negative liberty is realized when one can say "I am a slave to no man."[53] Both positive liberty and negative liberty are present in the dichotomy of freedom I have proposed. They exist in both the individual and communal aspects of liberty. I go as far as to argue they're essential components that are inseparable from this notion of freedom understood via the story of the connected self. In this reality, in which we are separated from and

---

v   I'd like to emphasize the choice to not act in a given situation as being an essential aspect of freedom. Some may claim that liberty inherently lies with action, but I argue that being coerced to act when you would otherwise choose not to would be a violation of your liberty. In this sense, liberty—and, by extension, freedom—requires the inherent presence of choice as well as the ability to act with minimal coercion.

connected to the world around us simultaneously, is the understanding that we, as individuals and as communities, have the autonomy to act in a way that affects not only other individuals directly, but society as a whole as well, even if the consequences of such actions are indirect or deferred. The effects of our actions can constitute either coercion or the removal of obstacles, on ourselves and/ or others. Therefore, for freedom to exist for all people, including ourselves, we must recognize that actions made on both the individual and collective levels can be affirmative and/or harmful.

> One [liberty] may abort another; one [liberty] may obstruct or fail to create conditions which make other [liberties], or a larger degree of freedom, or [liberties] for other persons, possible; positive and negative [liberty] may collide; the [liberty] of the individual or the group may not be fully compatible with a full degree of participation in a common life, with its demands for co-operation, solidarity, and fraternity.[54]

On the individual level, liberty is recognized as the power of individuals to act free from constraint instilled by others (negative liberty) and as the power of individuals to act upon self-determination to advance their potential (positive liberty). Likewise, liberty is recognized on the collective level as the power of a community to act free from the constraints imposed by the will of its people, with respect to its people domestically[vi] (negative liberty), and

---

vi   Actions pertaining to that given society, not interactions with other collective entities as in an international or global aspect.

as the power of a community to act according to the will of its people, with respect to its people domestically (positive liberty). Thusly, freedom can be broken down visually into four quadrants of liberties, each of which are necessary for freedom—the appropriate balance of these liberties within a society—to exist.

Starting from the top left (see page 103), the first quadrant is the negative liberty of the collective: the liberty of a community or governing body, as a singular entity, to act without being coerced by the will of its people[vii] in any given situation. At first, this liberty may seem counterintuitive to being a vital part of a free society. But there are times when the majority, as exemplified earlier, when exploring the story of the whole, can be wrong. Let's say a democratic majority in a society decides it's not comfortable living in the same state with a certain group of people who have a distinct ethnic background, and that majority votes to deport everyone of that ethnicity. If a free society was bound to always follow the will of the majority, then in this scenario, these people, even if they haven't done anything wrong or broken any laws, would be deported. I would argue that any society that does this is not free but prejudiced and exploitive. The power of collective "positive" liberty—to act according to the will of the people—would completely overpower the liberty of a

---

vii   For all intents and purposes, the notion of "the will of the people" should be understood in the context of a democratic society where majority rules. Therefore, you should read this line interchangeably with "the will of the majority."

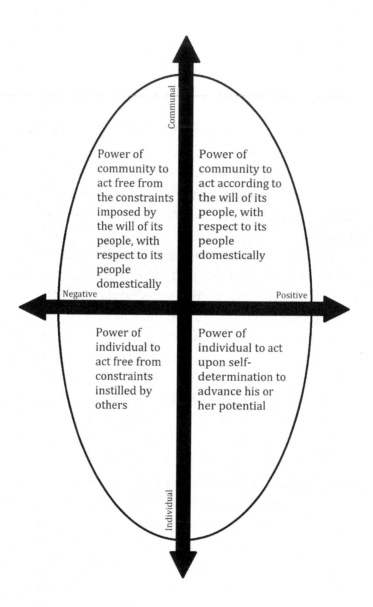

community to act on principle to protect the freedom of all people in that society. In this scenario, I would argue that it is the obligation of the collective—the governing body—to reject the will of the majority in the interest of preserving a status of freedom. If, through the course events, the will of the majority is continually affirmed (right or wrong) to the point where the governing body *never* acts in principle, regardless of circumstance, the point of convergence on the quadrant visual shifts too far towards positive collective liberty. This leaves collective negative liberty dominated and void of practical application.

The second quadrant, moving clockwise, is the positive liberty of the collective: the liberty of a community or governing body, as a singular entity, to act according to the will of its people. This liberty is vital to sovereignty and, thus, vital to freedom. If a democratic majority rightfully decides it wants to spend surplus tax revenue on a public works program—let's say, to build new bridges and replace antiquated ones—the governing body should listen and execute this idea in the interest of freedom. How free would this society be if the members of its governing body replied by rejecting this proposal and decided to spend tax revenue differently, like building new sports stadiums instead, even though the majority did not vote for such a course of action? Surely if members of the government felt this was a more rational investment, they'd make their case and urge a re-vote instead of just taking the decision into their own hands. To make this decision unilaterally would result in collective negative liberty completely overpowering collective positive liberty.[viii] The majority may not always be right, but there are many cases when it is and/or when a majority decision should stand in the interest of freedom. If, through the course events, the will of the majority is *never* acted upon, society ceases to be democratic in principle; the rights of "the people" are nonexistent. The point of convergence in the quadrant visual shifts too far towards negative liberty and/or too far towards individual liberty, leaving collective positive liberty dominated and void of practical application.

The third quadrant is individual positive liberty: the liberty of an individual to act according to his or her own will. Many would also refer to this liberty as "self-determination." Individual choice and being able to advance oneself as one sees fit is a principle the United States, in particular, was founded upon. In order for a society to be free, an individual must be able to exercise his or her autonomy. Should obstacles imposed by others prevent this liberty for certain individuals—let's say, by society deciding to eliminate all public schools so those with less money have no practical right to get a proper education free of tuition, in order to advance their own potential—one could argue that society ceases to be free. How free can a society be free if it doesn't allow tangible, practical opportunities for its citizens? In this case, the negative liberty of wealthy individu-

viii   And, I would argue, it would result in the liberty of this individual, who unilaterally makes this decision on behalf of the collective, overpowering collective positive liberty as well.

als—to not be coerced into paying taxes in order to fund public education—and the liberty of the collective who made the decision to eliminate public education would overpower and dominate the positive liberty of others. The members of a society's civic population must be afforded real choices and real opportunities in the interest of freedom. If, through the course of events, an individual or a select group of individuals is *never* able to make a practical choice to advance himself or herself through his or her own free will, then the point of convergence on the quadrant visual shifts too far towards the individual negative liberty of others, and possibly too far towards the positive liberty of the collective. Individual positive liberty is left dominated, void of practical application.

The fourth and final quadrant is individual negative liberty: the liberty of an individual to act free from coercion perpetrated by others. Acknowledging individual negative liberty ensures that practices like slavery or compulsory child labor are made illegal. There are necessary limits on an individual's liberty to act free from the influence of others. Absolute individual negative liberty would mean an individual could be allowed to commit murder without punishment, which is obviously an irrational practice for any free society. However, the limits a governing body should place on individuals to restrict them from committing certain acts should only go so far in any society that truly considers itself free.

The United States once tried to limit individual negative liberty by curbing individuals' behavior of consuming alcohol via prohibition. This social experiment failed miserably, and the constitutional amendment that authorized Prohibition was repealed shortly thereafter. When a collective goes too far in restricting what individuals can and cannot do, freedom ceases to exist. Even if a majority finds a certain act irrational or undesirable, a majority should not always be allowed to prohibit such acts in the interest of freedom. For if an individual is prohibited choice, that individual is nothing more than a slave. If, through the course events, an individual or a select group of individuals is *never* allowed to act free from coercion of others, then the point of convergence on the quadrant visual shifts too far towards collective liberty. The negative liberty of the individual is dominated, void of practical application.

On this point, I argue that there are conditions of individual liberty that are *always* present where freedom exists. When Thomas Jefferson wrote in the Declaration of Independence, "We hold these truths to be self-evident, that all men are created equal, that they are endowed by their Creator with certain unalienable rights, that among these are life, liberty and the pursuit of happiness,"[55] he was referring to the essentials of individual liberty that are inherent in any true balance that constitutes freedom. In this balance, individuals do have inalienable rights that must be upheld. Or at the very least, there are no grounds for a collective authority to prohibit them. Isaiah Berlin also speaks of such liberties in a more abstract, theoretical nature:

> If I wish to preserve my liberty, it is not enough to say that it must not be violated unless someone

or other... authorizes its violation. I must establish a society in which there must be some frontiers of freedom which nobody should be permitted to cross. Different names or natures may be given to the rules that determine these frontiers: they may be called natural rights, or the word of God, or natural law, or the demands of utility or the 'permanent interests of man'; I may believe them to be valid a priori, or assert them to be my own ultimate ends, or the ends of my society or culture. What these rules or commandments will have in common is that they are accepted so widely, and are grounded so deeply in the actual nature of men as they have developed throughout history, as to be, by now, an essential part of what we mean by being a normal human being. Genuine belief in the inviolability of a minimum extent of individual liberty entails some such absolute stand.[56]

These essential liberties include an individual's right to life, personal expression, and pursuit of happiness. Individual liberty becomes subservient to forces of collective control, should any one of these liberties be suppressed by the force of a collective authority, rather than an equal yet opposite force on the same level to enforce balance. After all, these individual liberties must be afforded to all individuals, not just some, in a free society. British philosopher John Stuart Mill, in his essay "On Liberty," outlined the reasons why these certain individual liberties must not be prohibited in such a free society. Mill hypothesized that even in a democratic society, the individual liberties most likely to be oppressed were those belonging to persons who expressed themselves in an unorthodox manner or in a manner that did not fit the expectations of a majority of the people.[57] He proposed that no society, democratic or not, has the right to oppress or subjugate such individuals if it is to rightfully call itself free, lest their expressions cause direct harm upon another individual. An injustice imposed by a democratic majority is just as bad as an injustice imposed by an autocratic dictator.[58] In summary, he makes three points that explain why:

1. Such expressions of individual liberty—what Mill called "uncustomary" thoughts and actions—may indeed be truly right in the divine or absolute sense. To prohibit such expressions would be an assertion of infallibility by the authorities that be. Since no person or group of people can be infallible, such prohibition would constitute a violation of freedom.[59]

2. Such expressions of individual liberty may pertain, at least in part, to what is true. To prohibit such expressions would disallow the ability to explore the status of what is considered true in pursuit of a new or greater truth. Should the ability for such exploration be made impossible, the prohibition of the expressions in question would constitute a violation of freedom.[60]

3. Such expressions of individual liberty may provide insights with which to analyze and critique

the status quo. To prohibit such expressions would create a form of undue prejudice, stemming from fear of what is not yet known. These expressions could also help form a fuller understanding of the doctrines that society holds true. Should the ability to understand the world in a different manner, in more than one way of thinking, be made impossible, the prohibition of the expressions in question would constitute a violation of freedom.[61]

Any form of suppression, as described above, by a democratic society would create, what Mill defined as, a tyranny of the majority—a condition in which a majority of people in a given society choose to utilize the liberties of the collective to dominate and suppress the liberties of select individuals or select groups of individuals.[62]

In a free society, no collective authority, democratic majority or not, has the right to violate these tenets of individual liberty. Such a violation would create a circumstance in which the balance of freedom becomes unstable and ceases to exist. That being said, we must be careful about what is considered an essential part of individual liberty. Acting rationally for one's self-interests in the name of individual liberty and freedom should not be confused with acting rationally for one's self-desires. There are certainly aspects of individualism that can be attained in a free society but aren't subject to the same protections as the inalienable liberties present in the balance of freedom. For example, there is no right or liberty for an individual to feel comfortable or self-assured and, therefore, prohibit the actions of others with whom he or she disagrees. Nor is there a right or liberty for an individual to be shielded from ideas or expressions with which he or she disagrees by banning them from society entirely. Nor is there a right or liberty for an individual to purchase or consume whatever he or she desires without limit.[ix] These may be perceived by some as individual rights, but they are not inalienable liberties granted to individuals; they are examples of dominating what is deemed to be inferior for the purpose of fulfilling individual desire for comfort. To mistake this rationality of domination for the rationality of individual liberty is to allow a society to exist under the false guise of "freedom." We must realize this and solidify our understanding of freedom as an extension of the connected self. If we fail to do so, it will be as John Stuart Mill concludes:

> The disposition of mankind, whether as rulers or as fellow citizens, to impose their own opinions and inclinations as a rule of conduct on others, is so energetically supported by some of the best and some of the worst feelings incident in human nature, that it is hardly ever kept under restraint by anything but want of power; and as the power is not declining, but growing, unless a strong bar-

---

ix This example, in particular, should be clarified: firms—groups of individuals recognized as a singular entity, like an individual, under the law—also should be included. In many cases, consumption and production are pursued limitlessly by firms (e.g., businesses, corporations) that have the means to pursue them, whereas an actual human individual is less likely to have the same resources.

rier of moral conviction can be raised against the mischief, we must expect, in the present circumstances of the world, to see it increase.[63]

In order for freedom to exist in a given society, all four quadrants of liberty must be present. When liberties are balanced—that is, when, through the course of events, the combination of liberties chosen to be upheld, protected, and exercised in their given circumstances to a point where an irrefutable margin of that society's citizens agree that such an amalgamation is appropriate and true—the status of "freedom" is attained. This model for freedom can be realized and practiced in more than one way. Organizational structures of power can be formal or informal, centralized or decentralized, local or national. The only unconditional requirement is that such a society has democratic principles of sovereignty, self-determination, and equality under the law. Any other form of governance that exercises authority without the consent of the people being governed will fail, inevitably, to be sustained, due to its inability to ensure the balance of liberties that is freedom. Many forms of national governance that have strayed away from the model of democracy[x] have succumbed to the political environment of control created by existing outside the metaphorical area in which freedom exists. Most examples, from nondemocratic monarchies to autocratic regimes of fascism or communism, failed

---

x Parliamentary, Republican, etc.; any type of model where the people have a direct say in lawmaking and execution of authority.

because the point of convergence in the quadrant visual strayed too far upward. They attempted to create a reality understood in terms of the story of the whole and ended up eliminating—either on purpose or inadvertently—many individual liberties. These examples resulted in collapse, usually due to revolution or forced reform on the existing system. Other examples, from over-expanding empires to newly formed, decentralized confederations, failed because the point of convergence drifted too far downward. So much power lay with individuals and small communities that unity among what was supposed to be one people was never achieved. These examples resulted in self-destruction, usually by infighting or being conquered by a stronger, unified force.

The extremes of both individualism and communalism are where the balance of liberties is lost and freedom ceases to exist. These powers of liberty become forces of control. The dichotomy of freedom between two forces of liberty, individual and collective, stop working together as one system and instead work against each other in a destructive manner for the purpose of one side dominating the other. Attempting to control human nature—individual or society—is unsustainable and with utter certainty will fail. Individuals are not meant to control societies, just as societies are not meant to control individuals. A balance between liberties is needed for freedom to exist and for society to thrive in peace. I therefore conclude that that freedom—the proper balance of individual, collective, positive, and negative liberties—is achieved when the following three statuses are present simultaneously:

1. When society, on both micro and macro levels, is agreed by the greatest percentage its citizens possible to be most just and tranquil.

2. When the power to choose is maximized for both individuals and society at large simultaneously.

3. When society at large does not violate or does not allow its citizens to violate the inalienable liberties that should be afforded to all individuals.

This reality requires compromise between the essential notions of individualism and communalism. Rules and regulations set by a democratic society for the purpose of ensuring that opportunity exists for the masses may be perceived by an individual who is negatively affected by such rules as a violation of his or her individual liberty. The bigger picture—the balance of freedom—should always be kept in mind. In this sense, the *absolute* notions of individual liberty—that any and all actions made by individual should be unrestricted short of direct physical injury upon another—*must* be violated to some extent in order for freedom to exist.[xi] Any one individual can find some fault with the laws established by a collective authority, but he or she can retain liberty, along with society at large, as long as the laws society puts in place do not prevent him or her from pursuing self-interest and do not constrain him or her from exercising expressions of individuality that do not directly harm another individual. Compromise requires the rejec-

---

xi   The same goes for the absolute notions of collective liberty as well.

tion of absolutist interpretations of what freedom means. Society must stand on principles that influence political decisions and reject a foundation based upon the desire to achieve an impossible reality. Within these principles is plenty of room for compromise, which is necessary for society to live peacefully and progress in its pursuit of true freedom and justice.

How does a nation achieve such a practical balance of liberties in the political sense and therefore secure freedom? How do we know what that balance looks like? I, or any other individual, cannot prescribe the exact sets of laws or statutes that will secure freedom for a given society. There are bound to be countless combinations of existing and new ideas that could work to achieve this balance. However, we can conclude, given what we've explored in this book thus far, that this balance will be reached through a combination of rational expectations, social obligations, legal parameters, and the like. These tangible expressions of a society's social contract are based on and directly tied to a society's identity, history, and guiding principles—society's ethos. And, as I proposed earlier in this book, a society's ethos is grounded in that society's environment.

This is where bioregionalism comes back into the discussion. If societal ethos is defined, at least in part, by a bioregion's environmental distinctions, thereby fundamentally differentiating societal ethos from one another on the bioregional level of ecological distinction, then the proper balance of liberties in a society needed to achieve freedom—which will be attained through a combination of the elements of that society's social contract, which are, in turn, based on that society's ethos—will be determined in part by that society's bioregion and fundamentally differentiated from societies in other bioregions. In our case, this means we can conclude that the appropriate balance of liberties needed to achieve freedom in Cascadia will be unique to us and fundamentally differentiated, to some extent, from the rest of the continent. To us, decisions made on the federal level in both the United States and Canada tend to default, a majority of the time, towards securing individual economic liberties rather than securing balance between individualism and collectivism, because the ethos (plural) of regions to our east tend to lean in such a manner relative to Cascadia. Likewise, to other regions in our two countries, some decisions we make collectively in the Cascadian region seem highly unorthodox because we tend to default towards securing a balance as it pertains to us, which can result in the dismantling of laws seen by others needed to preserve social order (e.g., doctor-assisted suicide, marijuana legalization) or in the creation of laws deemed by others to be an intrusion on individual liberty (e.g., more-impactful environmental protection statutes).

When you look at the big picture, you realize our statuses quo are regional by design of nature. The way things are in Cascadia does not create the same condition as the way things are in a neighboring region or a region on the other side of the continent; these conditions are unique to our regional ethos. And if our present condition is unique to our regional ethos, then our laws and our balance of freedom must be formed to match it. As our condition fluctuates with time in Cascadia, so must our balance of liberties be adjusted and maintained to ensure freedom and harmony. We can do this region-ally, as such a balance is regional by nature. We cannot continue to try to achieve the same goal on our current federal levels in the United States and Canada without reform. We must understand our present conditions on regional levels, along with the balances of liberties that derive from them. Our social contract will need to be different from the current status quo—inherently locked in with the rest of the United States and Canada—should we truly wish to secure freedom for our society.[xii] And because our social contract is rightly determined by us—the people who live here and wish to exercise sov-ereignty and self-determination—it is our moral right and obligation to determine this status of freedom ourselves, without being controlled by non-Cascadian influences.

In Cascadia, our understanding of freedom and our status quo extends to the environment that surrounds

---

xii   I do not deny the possibility that other regions' ethos (plural) are compatible with each other, as far as they can ex-ist desirably within a wider system. I cannot make such a case for any other region because I do not share or subscribe to the bioregional nationhood of any other region. In Cascadia's case, as is mentioned numerous times in this book, we are a region split significantly into two different countries. The likelihood, therefore, that Cascadia can exist as a single entity to the same capacity of compatibility with other regions under *one* larger system is all but impossible, given the existence of both Canada and the United States.

us. The living communities that exist in nature are part of us; we take into account their right to exist, free from overconsumption or exploitation. Be it through the rationality of sustainability or conservation, we understand that consumption has an effect on us and the region in which we live. We often seek to preserve our surroundings in which others, as well as future generations, may thrive. The strength of this morality is a profound phenomenon in Cascadia, which stems from the region itself. We seek to be true inhabitants of our communities, not mere occupants. The earth as a body, which needs to be nourished and cared for in order to survive, is a metaphor we live by. It's a principal epistemological concept that we use to understand who we are on the most basic level.[64] Each of these notions can be part of Cascadia's new narrative that defines our society and differentiates us from the perpetual consumptive nature that prevails in the United States and Canada—Cascadia's story of balance and coexistence versus the American dream of economic domination and accumulation of power and wealth. In this juxtaposition, Cascadia's story is that of a free nation; the other is that of exploitive and selfish empires.

Of course, I do not claim these negative qualities are the only ones that exist or are espoused in the United States and/or Canada. Both countries also pride themselves on notions of service, expanding hope for those who have little and being the vanguard of righteousness and democracy. But the nature of consumption and tendencies towards radical individualism inherent in the stories of these two countries, whose ethos are dominated by regions closer to the East Coast, is the crux of the differentiation between the rest of the continent and Cascadia. In Cascadia, the basis for our perception of freedom is through a balance that works for us as a whole, through an affirmation of our entire living system, its natural rights, and our will to ensure its optimal existence through conservation, innovation, and other sustainable means. We are beginning to realize that our balance of freedom is determined by our ethos and our environment, distinctly and fundamentally different from the balance of regions to our east.

> The current major societal institutions in the West—government, economic, and religion—all support the assumption that the liberty, gratification and salvation of the individual human person is the appropriate view of who we are in the scheme of things. This is diametrically opposed to how we should think of ourselves within an ecological world view. It is impossible to imagine us acting differently—acting as "ecological citizens"—unless we internalize ecological values.[65][xiii]

Cascadia is a region out of balance. We have an intense feeling something is fundamentally wrong with our

---

[xiii]   This quote from Sallie McFague paraphrases a section from Seppo Kjellberg's book *Urban Eco Theology* (Utrecht: International Books, 2000).

political statuses quo that is leading to unprecedented political gridlock, inaction, apathy, confusion, and widespread disapproval. For an entire generation of Americans and Canadians born within the last decade or two, this reality is all they have ever known. We still love our country, and we appreciate the sacrifices made by those who came before us and how fortunate we are today, relative to generations past, but the presence of something fundamentally wrong in our status quo is inescapable. And regardless of our affinities towards the idea of what America or Canada should be, we feel the weight of the inevitable, should we continue on our current courses. Something must give; something must change on a fundamental level.

I am one who agrees with these sentiments. I am also one who believes fundamental change is both possible and realistically attainable. The most difficult part, besides the logistics of achieving fundamental change once a direction is chosen, is for us to understand what the root causes of these problems really are. I do not claim there is one magical solution that will be the key to solving all of our problems. I do, however, believe that there are key problems caused, perpetuated, made inscrutable, or made unworkable by our intrinsic regional natures in the United States and Canada. These problems result in the potential for liberties and freedom to be diminished for Cascadians. It is my belief that identifying these problems and their correlation with bioregionalism is vital to achieving beneficial, lasting change for all. There's a common cliché: "Knowing is half the battle." If we know what these root problems are and how they're affected, we can know and evaluate our possibilities.

5. OUR STATUS OF AFFAIRS AND POLITICAL INEVITABILITY

We in Cascadia have reached a crucial point in history for our society. Most of us haven't realized just how crucial it really is or why it is, but we most certainly feel—at least subliminally—that we have reached a point of no return. Something monumental needs to change; our systems of governance, discourse, and decision making on a societal level, on both sides of the international border, cannot continue existing in their current manifestations with their current demeanor. While gridlock and inaction pervades in Washington, DC, allowing the crooked practices of the most powerful corporate institutions to continue largely unchallenged, public policy favoring corporate exploitation and institutionalism expands its influence in Ottawa. The intensely individualistic and consumption-based nature of exercising liberty dominates our federal statuses quo to the benefit of the most powerful on the eastern half of the continent. As a result, resources and means are shrinking, and we, as Cascadians, are left fractured, frustrated, and unable to exercise publically based solutions that work for us, regardless of our animosity or sympathy towards the intentions behind our federal institutions of power. This goes beyond problems with democratic process or bureaucracy. Our "national" identities as Americans and Canadians have become irreversibly flawed and incompatible with Cascadia. Our collective liberties as Cascadians are being suppressed, leaving our region out of balance. Our ability to bring ourselves back into balance is thwarted as a result of non-Cascadian influences dominating federal priorities. Our systems of government, as a consequence, are inadequate to meet our needs. Treating the symptoms of our flawed bodies of governance may temporarily and superficially take care of what we think is ailing our status quo. But no matter how many elections we have in the near future, they will not fix the fundamental issues plaguing Cascadia.

We're living through a period of mistreatment by non-Cascadian influences. The starkest examples can currently be witnessed by corporate interests taking advantage of our environment and geography. Building coal-train routes and export centers through Cascadia has been proposed so mining companies, based outside of our region, can sell cheap fuel to Asian markets, thereby increasing global carbon dioxide emissions by staggering amounts.[66] Oil-train routes and port terminals are already used by foreign companies, with more planned to be built.[67] The Canadian federal government has pushed for a tar sands oil pipeline to be built through British Columbia[68] against the will of First Nations and the general population of that province[69], so non-Cascadian, resource-based corporations can sell fossil fuel to Asian markets. The remnants of past resource exploitation projects in British Columbia remain an ongoing threat to countless acres of forest and waterways.[70] Each time, our land is used—or desired to be used—not for our benefit but for the benefit of outside corporations. Each time, our region and its environment—the surroundings we revere, regardless of our feelings towards these programs—is put into harm's way and in danger of permanent damage, for the sake of others' profits. And each time, the governments that are supposed to look out for us do nothing, do too little to protect our interests, or encourage these projects in the name of economic benefit for Canada or the United States as a whole. Our say and our will as Cascadians, ultimately, do not matter, regardless of our opinions. What is "good" for the most powerful east of the Continental Divide will reign, whatever the circumstances may be.

On our current trajectory through the course of events, it is inevitable that a time will come in the relatively near future when the following things will happen: First, the desire and/or expectation for the consumption-based ways of life that are prevalent throughout most of the United States and Canada—living with more than one would realistically ever need for the sake of social convention or a sense of entitlement—will collide with the reality that our resources, which so many assume to be plentiful, to sustain such ways of life will become severely limited, due to overconsumption and a lack of replenishment. When that happens, an insurmountable number of people will suffer socially and economically, though they will have done their best their entire lives to work hard and earn what they have honestly.

Second, the governing and economic powers that be in the United States and Canada will look to preserve these ways of life and the social order that comes with it at nearly any cost. Surely some progress will be made to introduce more sustainable ways of living as well, but the majority who feel as if they are unjustly punished in a cruel world will argue, successfully, to use the means at our countries' disposal to restore reality to what it used to be, however impractical that may be.

Third, the dominant governing and economic powers in the United States and Canada, residing east of the Continental Divide, will look to the last region with relatively plentiful resources to exploit: Cascadia. When that happens, our geography and our resources won't just be used to allow others to profit, as they are now; our resources will be extracted and consumed at alarming rates under the argument that such actions are good and/or necessary for the rest of the country. The federal governments of the United States and Canada will strengthen their partnerships with the most powerful economic forces and proceed accordingly to the interests of the many, ironically and effectively working against our common interests as Cascadians. This exploitation will be welcomed and cheered by those who don't live in our region. There will, of course, be promises made to extract our resources wisely, with respect to our surroundings. But in the end, demand from and profit for those to our east will determine how much we lose. If a man-made disaster strikes, causing permanent damage to our environment and our economy, there will no doubt be sympathies and efforts to fix it, ensuring any damage is paid for, as if we can be reimbursed for damage caused to material goods. But any long-lasting effects after the immediate damage subsides will largely be ignored as our regional society endures suffering, as with any other similar occurrence in our recent history.

One need only look to the ecosystem[71] and local economy[72] of Valdez, Alaska, or the indigenous communities of northern British Columbia to rightfully assume this. I fear that by the time it takes the rest of our two countries to evolve socially past the desire or expectation to continue overconsumption, it will be too late for us. Our environment will permanently change for the worse. It is at this point that we, as Cascadians, will truly and undeniably lack liberty and freedom. Cascadia will no longer be an equal partner within our two countries but a subservient subject. Our desire to preserve and conserve our surroundings—the place we live and call home—will collide against the will of most others in the United States and Canada. And if history is any indicator, we'll be on the losing side.

Make no mistake; I am not alluding or arguing that we should stop any and all resource-based economy in Cascadia. Utilizing natural resources to sustain human communities is part of life. It always has been and always will be. I am also not alluding or arguing that we should give up every social or economic aspect of our lives that we identify as American or Canadian. I am simply arguing that there will come a point where non-Cascadian influences in the United States and Canada will attempt to overwhelm our collective will and means as Cascadians, regardless of our sympathies or political ideologies, unless something fundamental changes about our status quo. For some in Cascadia, the point when and where exploitation of our land has become intolerable has already arrived; the number of those who agree will only grow.

Having conjectured what is yet to come, it is rational to ask the question, "Why can't we simply fix the current systems of governance so our future is safeguarded?" Or to put it another way, "Why can't we simply optimize our current systems of governance to the point where we can amend or change the laws that are overwhelming our regional collective liberties and bring our society back into balance?" The answer to these questions is inseparably connected to bioregionalism: the natural, regional ethos that make up the American or Canadian identity and guiding principles are irreconcilably clashing with each other in Washington, DC, or Ottawa.

Think of it this way: the United States or Canada is a team made up of a select few individuals. These individuals are the regions that make up both of our countries. The team is playing a game in which they play by themselves and compete to achieve the ideal result of whatever that game is. For instance, if we were to imagine this game as an obstacle course, the team's goal would be to work together to complete the course with maximum efficiency and as few errors as possible. Within this game, there are resources each team member can use, depending on who she or he is. Ideally, each team member should be able to use his or her resources to benefit the entire team, including himself or herself. This game also has rules by which the team has to abide. The rules can be changed, if need be, as long as a majority of team members agree to whatever change is proposed and any change does not destroy the integrity of the game. Ideally, each team member should be able to conform to the rules without having to play at a disadvantage and, thusly, the team should be able to perform as one coherently synced group of individuals.

If we use this metaphor to understand our current status quo as a country—either the United States or Canada—we see that our regions (team members) have a goal of utilizing its resources. These resources may be natural, material, or of an intangible, actionable nature, such as an act, talent, or service committed by an individual or group of individuals, so that society as a whole is optimized in such a way that individuals can thrive coherently as they see fit. The country will thrive as a result of these optimal conditions. The rules in this metaphor should be understood as the laws created by the federal legislators—they can be changed, if need be, provided that a majority agree with such changes.

Now let's apply this metaphor to our status quo. The team is stalled or working inefficiently. Some team members are unable to perform optimally because their resources have been utilized, some team members' talents are stunted by the rules of the game, and just about every team member sees fit to change the rules of the game in one way or another. The problem is that team members can't widely agree on rule changes. The only ones that a majority finds acceptable severely limit one or more team members in the minority from performing optimally. Everyone agrees that such a rule change could help the team as a whole in the immediate future, but it would cause certain individuals to sacrifice far too much, endangering the team's chances of being able to compete as a whole later on in the game. This is where Cascadia is now—we've hit a point in "the game" where our region and its individuals cannot perform optimally. In order to fix this, laws need to be changed in one way or another. The specifics of what those laws are and what about them needs to be changed depends on a complex web of overlapping circumstances and differing rationalities.

Each region will have a unique foundation of identity, values, principles, and resources from which to analyze the status quo. Within each region should be a relatively coherent spectrum of ideas, opinions, and rationalities that are native to this unique foundation. Ideally, in countries such as the United States and Canada, these spectrums, represented federally by elected officials of the people, should be reconcilable in a single federal system. That way, debate, consideration, and compromise should be attained in order to change the laws that all must abide by without causing detriment to any one region or its foundation. This ideal perhaps was attainable at one time in the past, when the United States' or Canada's constitutional documents were formed around an ephemeral reality specific to a finite collection of geography and naturally influenced ethos of the time. I argue, however, that this ideal—the ability to reach federal reconciliation under our current makeups—can no longer be achieved in the eyes of Cascadians, due to our natural ethos being most divergent, in principle and in strength of representation, from the conglomeration of ethos that make up either the United States or Canada as a whole. We could try to understand this concept by looking at a Venn diagram, which is used to show the relations between a finite collection of sets:

Region 1 (dominant ethos)   Region 4
Region 2   Region 5
Region 3   Region 6 (most divergent ethos)

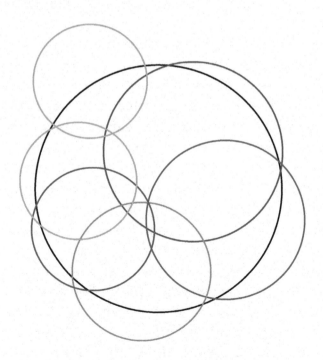

The large black circle in the middle represents the conglomeration of regional ethos that is the country's identity. Think of it as the American or Canadian identity. Each region within that country will have its own ethos, represented by the colored circles, which contributes to the country's identity. The more influential regions naturally will be more dominant and fit well within the country's identity. Any divergence—aspects of regional identity that cannot be considered part of the country's collective identity—will fall outside of the black circle in the middle. Each region is bound to have a little bit of divergence, as no region perfectly represents the country as a whole. It is likely, therefore, that no one region will ever fit entirely within the black circle in the middle. If any region exists primarily outside the black circle, its ethos is poorly represented in the country. As a result, such a region will not be able to perform optimally according to its own population. In such a circumstance, the population of a divergent region, if it wishes to not be divergent, would have to decide to consciously act in a manner inconsistent with its natural identity in order to conform to the identity of the country. This is an irrational and unsustainable option that uses the same rationality as a majority of people telling another individual to change who she or he is—to not be herself or himself—because it's inconvenient or discomforting for everyone else.

The option the country has as a whole, then, if it wishes to limit the divergence of such a region, would be for the other regions to willingly go against their own natural identities to an extent in order accommodate the divergent region. This is also an irrational and unsustainable option that can cause backlash among the populations of each of these regions, which risks limiting the common points of association between the regional identities to become too small, causing the black circle in the middle to shrink to a point where multiple regions are primarily divergent. This would only accentuate non-optimal conditions for the country. The only other options left for the country as a whole is to attempt forcible change of the divergent region, which would result in the blatant and irrefutable suppression of freedom for that region, or to let the divergent region go so it is no longer part of the country.

If we use this same Venn diagram model and use it to map out the relationships between the regional ethos (plural) within the United States and Canada, along with the relationship between the countries as wholes, it would look something like the diagram on the following page.[i]

The circles represent the ethos of each bioregion existing within the United States and Canada, along with the conglomerations of ethos that constitute the United

---

i   This diagram's labels refer to the bioregions as labeled in the map shown earlier in this book. Since this diagram compares the relationships of the ethos themselves—comparing the similarities of ecological and intangible aspects of the societies that reside in them—they are not sized by population. Furthermore, this is not a perfect representation but an attempt at an accurate one.

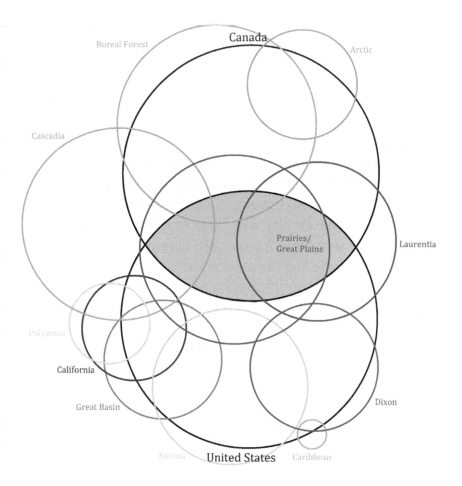

*Circles are not scaled to population

States and Canada.[ii] The shaded part in the middle represents the similar aspects between the American and Canadian identities. Both Laurentia (which contains cities like Boston, New York, Montreal, Toronto, and Chicago) and the Prairies (which contain cities like Calgary, Edmonton, Denver, Oklahoma City, Kansas City, Minneapolis, and Winnipeg) are very well represented in both the American and Canadian identities. The characteristics and ways of life of these two regions are essential to the identities of our two countries. In Canada, the other regions of influence are the boreal forest, which spans much of the northern part of the continent, and the Arctic. These two regions are sparsely populated but play a key role in understanding Canada's resource-based economy and affinity with "the North." In the United States, several other regions also have influence in contributing to the identity of America: Dixon (also known as "Dixie" or "the South"), Sonora (west Texas, New Mexico, Arizona), the Great Basin (Utah, Nevada), and California. The Caribbean (south Florida, Puerto Rico), the boreal forest/Arctic (Alaska), and Polynesia (Hawaii) also play a part in America's identity, but their anomalous statuses,

---

ii   Other artificial regional influences also exist in the United States and Canada—Texas and Quebec are two of the most obvious examples. These identities most certainly exist and are legitimate, but they're not founded upon the natural ethos of the regions in which each resides. That is, each of these areas would blend in with the rest of the their respective bioregions if it weren't for some characteristics (e.g., Quebec's French influence or Texas's initial independence from both the United States and Mexico) introduced as a result of historical circumstance.

relative to the other bioregions in the country, make it difficult to judge just how divergent they may or may not be. One could certainly make an argument that one or more should be understood as divergent regions within the United States. The last bioregion, represented in both the United States and Canada, is Cascadia. With its distinctive ethos, values of balance over consumption, and reverence of distinct natural surroundings, it most certainly stands out in both the United States and Canada as being in a unique circumstance. It also has become more divergent from both the American and Canadian identities naturally with time and more noticeably with our current circumstances, both economic and social.

When these regional ethos (plural) come together in assembly in either Ottawa or Washington, DC, represented by legislators elected by the people, they clash. Representatives from Georgia or Alabama, regardless of their political party, are going to understand and experience the world in a different way from representatives in Ohio, South Dakota, Utah, or California. Members of Parliament representing Nova Scotia or New Brunswick are going to have a very different outlook than members from Saskatchewan or Alberta, regardless of political party as well. This is the effect of bioregionalism in a nutshell. Ideally, enough commonplace can be found between regional ethos (plural), and compromises can be reached for the sake of good governance. If such compromises are in-line with the identity of the country as a whole, they should be met with majority approval. However, this majority approval may be opposed primarily by a divergent region. This is a phenomenon we're witnessing in Canada; policies have been endorsed or passed in Ottawa to the approval of many but to the ire of one region in particular.[iii] Such compromises can also be met with majority disapproval if they are not in line with the country's identity. This dissaproval, which is what's happening in the United States currently, happens when the level of commonality between the regions has shrunk to a point where only the more-extreme viewpoints on the federal spectrum of politics are represented.[iv]

When a country overexpands geographically to include multiple bioregions, it runs the risk of incorporating too many points of reference when trying to identify the commonalities between the naturally influenced ethos (plural) between them. Too many bioregions results in not enough commonalities needed for a democracy to function optimally. "The middle"—those less affiliated with any given political ideology and more-driven by their everyday experiences, which is influenced by the environment in which they live—is different, depending on what region you're in. Commonplace between regional identities in the political sense is then found with each regional ethos' compatibility with partisan ideology. When the level on commonality between the regions

iii I reference specifically the endorsement of the Enbridge Pipeline from the Canadian federal government among majority opposition from the people of British Columbia as a prominent and recent example.
iv Other factors, such a gerrymandering, have unquestionably played a part in accentuating this phenomenon.

shrinks too much, partisan gridlock ensues. The only way to move past it is if a single political party gains enough of a majority to effectively dominate minority influence in the federal legislative bodies. And I hope we can agree that if it takes an overwhelming majority by one party just to get the political system working as it was designed to work, there is little doubt that a fundamental change is needed.

We don't often think of federal politics from a regional perspective, but this is what happens when lawmakers and governing officials assemble in Ottawa or Washington, DC. Each country is experiencing a different phenomenon due to the effects of bioregionalism, but the results unto the Cascadian region and its people are the same in either case—our ethos is poorly represented in the outcomes of these phenomena due to our divergence from the American or Canadian norms. Our region is succumbing to the will of the others. By the standards I have proposed in this book, these results do not comprise the level of freedom we need as a region in order to thrive as we see fit. The other regions in our two countries will not simply change their ways to accommodate us; likewise, we cannot continue yielding our will indefinitely for the sake of federal cohesion.

So again, we come back to our original inquiry: why can't we just fix our current federal systems so they work for us as Cascadians as well as everyone else? Due to the effects unto our political systems pertaining to bioregionalism, which I have described in this chapter, I argue the fundamental changes we need as Cascadians, to the American and Canadian federal systems, are highly unlikely to occur for the following three reasons:

1. Effective Cascadian representation in the American and Canadian federal governments, to the point where the level of freedom we need is secured, is, for all practical purposes, impossible.

2. The unity across each country needed to pass fundamental reform, such as a constitutional amendment, for the purpose of securing the level of freedom we need as Cascadians, is, for all practical purposes, impossible.

3. The international border between the United States and Canada is a permanent barrier to securing the unity and the level of freedom we need as Cascadians in order to thrive as we see fit.

I argue it is, therefore, impractical for us as Cascadians to achieve the fundamental changes we need in order to thrive within our current federal systems of representation and governance in the United States and Canada. I wish to explore each of these reasons in greater detail before I come to any specific conclusion of what must be done instead.

Regarding the practical impossibility of effective Cascadian representation, let's start with the situation in the United States. The most noticeable fundamental flaw that inhibits Cascadia, in the system of representation the United States currently has, is that it operates on a two-party federal system. Both parties must de facto represent all parts of the country, regardless of bioregional differences. Major alternative parties that can actually compete with the two biggest parties are essential for better representation of the general populous in any democratic political system. Life is not black and white, red or blue, day or night. The issues that face the country are incredibly complex and require more than just one set of opposing ideas to solve them. In the United States, a third party with the ability to compete and realistically hold power would diversify discourse and embolden the exchange of ideas. It is naïve to think that multiple-party systems or more representative bodies in general will completely eliminate pettiness and inflamed rhetoric. Such strategies play to the emotions of voters, which is in the very nature of politics and will always be present in any form of democratic representation. However, it's hard to imagine Congress in Washington, DC, being as gridlocked and ineffective as it is now with more than two legitimate options to lead a federal agenda.

When it comes to electing a head of state, the Electoral College all but guarantees one of two candidates will ever have a realistic chance of winning in any given election; after all, there are a total of just 538 votes, and almost every state grants its vote total in bulk to the candidate who wins a plurality of votes. Voting for a third alternative presidential candidate is practically the same as handing your vote to whichever of the two major-party candidates you dislike the most. Third-party candidates for president have managed to acquire a significant percentage of the popular vote in the past, but the most electoral votes any of them has ever earned resulted in just 24% of the total amount available.[v]

In Congress, it was common for third-party members to hold a handful of seats in the House and Senate prior to the 1950s, but no third parties have ever been able to amount to the size of the Democrats or the Republicans in either chamber since the formation of the Republican Party. In fact, since the end of the Civil War, the most seats any third party has held in Congress was just 6% of the total amount of seats available.[vi] A significant third party in Congress might cause the legislative branch in Washington, DC, to diversify, work together, and compromise on behalf of the country far more than we see now. In fact, there have been calls for a third party to enter Congress or even the White House from nearly every region in the country. So why hasn't a stable third party been able to gain traction and win enough votes around the country to have members elected to Congress or even win the presidency? After all, voters not affiliated with either the Democratic or Republican parties outnumber those who have registered with either one of them. The answer pertains to the effects of bioregionalism—the regional diversity of the United States effectively prevents any third party from gaining significant influence.

---

v   John Breckenridge, a member of the Southern Democrat Party, earned 72 of 303 electoral votes in 1860, right before the South attempted to secede from the Union upon the election of Abraham Lincoln.

vi   The People's Party (Populists) held 27 total seats in Congress (5 Senate, 22 House) by the end of the 55th Congress in March 1899.

Third parties thrive on representing what I like to call "unclaimed political territory"—the lesser-represented ideological areas of the political spectrum that the two biggest parties tend to neglect or in which they are weakest. In the United States, such unclaimed political territory differs from region to region due to bioregionalism. If a unique environment directly influences a unique ethos, and a unique ethos influences a unique spectrum of politics, then there will be regional differentiation between these spectrums. And if third parties thrive on capitalizing on unclaimed political territory within a political spectrum, then a third party can only be truly competitive on a federal level if such unclaimed political territory is unified throughout the country. For each of the reasons pertaining to bioregionalism we have explored in this book, I argue that the unclaimed political territory in the United States is not unified. And because it is not unified, any attempt to create a sustainable, federal third-party movement has failed, in large part, as a result.

The two major parties have been able to co-opt different third-party movements, which originate from trying to take advantage of unclaimed political territory in different geographic regions, and adapt. For example, the largest third-party movement to make so much as a dent in Congress' two-party establishment since the end of the Civil War was the People's Party (also known as the Populist Party) in the late nineteenth and early twentieth centuries. It grew out of the largely agrarian South and Great Plains regions, spreading to the Midwest at its peak point of influence. It began with farmers and people in rural areas trying to fill a void pertaining to agrarian issues in politics, which the Democrats and Republicans were not adequately filling. But as it spread and began seeing its members elected to state legislatures and the United States Congress, it started having trouble resolving regional diversities in party philosophy. Since its existence was largely due to economic issues, primarily regarding agrarian communities, members from different regions began inserting other philosophies into their personal platforms in an attempt to break the stronghold of the Democratic Party at the time, which was the major party that held the strongest representation of said areas. Some Populists in the South outwardly supported white supremacy, while more liberal Populists in the Great Plains and Midwest denounced such beliefs. Some state parties in the South tried to form alliances with their Republican counterparts to combat Democratic Party control.

In the end, the party owed its existence to the gap it filled in unclaimed political territory, which only existed in certain regions of the country. Such a platform that spoke to the concerns of primarily agrarian areas had little chance of succeeding in the Mid-Atlantic or Northeast. This allowed the federal Democratic Party— the party that was much closer aligned to the Populists' economic platform—to co-opt the movement and adapt many of that party's ideas into its own. As the Democratic Party had long held the federal infrastructure and influence that the People's Party never had, it successfully began to fill the void that the Populists attempted to fill in certain regions of the country.

For a more recent example, we can turn to the Tea Party movement that began shortly after the election of President Obama. Spurred by conservatives angry with increased government spending and potential tax increases, a conservative- and libertarian-based movement began that outwardly and vehemently rejected further expansion of the federal government's power and influence. Other domestic issues of a social nature took a backseat as federal spending and the federal debt took center stage. Seeing opportunity, wealthy members of the Republican Party, most notably Charles and David Koch, made significant investments in expanding the movement, funding it, and getting Republicans on board. After all, the Republican Party had the federal infrastructure to legitimize the movement across the country; ignoring it would likely lead to a split of right-of-center votes, which would result in more left-of-center politicians elected to office due to the United States' plurality-wins voting model.[vii] While this movement stood a better chance of becoming an actual third-party influence because its concerns were so specific and universal among right-of-center voters, such as federal spending, deficits, and the debt, it quickly became fractured as a mix of libertarian-minded people who couldn't care less about social issues, of socially conservative independents who conformed this movement to match their own values, and of members of the Republican Party. This fractured Tea

---

vii   Some states do have a run-off model, but most award an election victory to the candidate which wins the most votes, even if it isn't a majority.

Party was not a legitimate alternative in several regions of the country, such as the Northeast and much of the West Coast. Without the systemic and financial assistance of the federal Republican Party, the Tea Party movement's stability and long-term viability remained questionable at best. Seeing a chance to expand its sphere of influence, the GOP acted quickly and co-opted the movement as part of its own, thus filling the void of ideological territory that this independent movement sought to occupy in multiple regions of the country. The result was a significant amount of Tea Party-affiliated Republicans winning elections in 2010. In both of these cases—the People's Party and the Tea Party—a legitimate third-party movement failed at becoming viable federally due to regional differences. The two-party system that continues to this day co-opted these movements as a result.

Subsequently, another fundamental flaw that prohibits more accurate democratic representation via third parties in the United States is that so much attention, emphasis, and power in American politics is at the federal level instead of local levels. There are many issues that are appropriately addressed at the federal level because their concerns affect the entire country, not just a specific region. Each federal party and its candidates need to speak to the issues that affect the entire country. Candidates from such a party should be able to run for the highest federal offices and have a legitimate chance at winning such positions.[viii] While such emphasis is usually

viii They shouldn't be members of minor movements that have no long-term credibility on the federal level.

appropriate for federal politics, the United States is not one cohesive nation. If third-party movements succeed by capitalizing on unclaimed political territory on a countrywide level, then it would come to reason that such third parties would address issues that affect the entire country and survive on political capital that is attained at the federal level. In order for that to occur, a country must be a cohesive nation with a common foundation for identity, culture, and politics. Thus, the United States' distinct regional composition is a major obstacle to any alternative-party movement and a detriment to effective representational democracy on the federal level.

The most glaringly obvious consequence of America's two-party federal system is that it fosters corruption in government institutions and, thusly, erodes the trust of the general populous in them. Because the two-party system denies any realistic opportunity for any other group to attain any political capital inherent in democratic representation in Congress, that capital—that power—is hoarded by just two parties. Competition is stifled, and the two major parties are allowed to hold a monopoly of power, inherently undue and unjustified. Much like economics, political monopolies keep the power in the hands of a few. This denies the people opportunity to ensure they're fairly and rightly represented in their own country. And any attempt to change the status quo is met with a more powerful resistance by those who hold the power. This plays into the very nature of corruption. Individuals working for the sake of greed—not money or power necessarily but more money or more power than one ought to have, from a non-subjective philosophical level—is what creates the opportunity for corruption. When those who have gained too much power see the potential for the loss of it, via direct or indirect circumstances, they will use their undue influence over others to ensure they keep it. And it's this exercise of power and corruption that leads to an imbalance of power, influence, and opportunity in society at large.

This progression results in fostering an either/or mentality in Congress between the two parties that hold the power. Worse still is that this mentality stunts the quality of debate when addressing very complex issues facing the country, which are anything but either/or. Look at almost any major issue facing Congress right now; you will find that a Democratic viewpoint and a Republican viewpoint dominate the debate. Yes, substantive discussions and ideas may come out of committees and commissions where debate is held among representatives who specialize in specific areas of policy and where testimony is given by the country's foremost experts on such policies. But when it comes time to bring the debate to the people on the floors of Congress to vote on a bill, the either/or mentality takes hold in the mind-sets of party leaders and dominates popular understanding of any given issue:

If bill X passes, it will legitimize "their" political capital and undermine "our" power; therefore, we need to frame the debate in a better light for "us," which gives "them" a greater chance at failure and "us" a greater chance at success. We need to shift the debate from "this, this, and this" to "our ideas (good) versus their ideas (bad)" because "we" want the political capital and the enhanced chances of winning the next election.

The hope is that compromise succeeds in these instances to merge ideas from both sides of the debate into one bill that considers the well-being of the many instead of the few, even if both parties find fault with it. Such compromise would come much more easily and frequently with more than two parties holding the political capital. The either/or mentality is far less likely to hold legitimacy if there are at least three options to choose from. However, as evidenced especially over the past few years, the prospect for power between two political monopolies can bring the country's business to a standstill and corrode debate away from actual issues to harmful disputes, which only de-legitimizes the American system of governance. The either/or mentality becomes the win/lose mentality— one where the personal security and sense of freedom of the people is subjected to perceived threats instead of expanded upon by broad-reaching ideas that can prove beneficial to the many. This is also what fosters polarization between the two parties, especially if one of the two is seen as becoming too powerful. The United States has had periods where a political party becomes the dominant majority by huge margins, and it is in these times where that party has claimed a mandate, for better or for worse (this aspect is irrelevant to the point), to move forward with their partisan agenda and little debate.

Unfortunately, such partisanship is inevitable in a country such as the United States; the more the general population grows in each region, the more distinct each regional foundation for politics solidifies, and the harder it becomes for the federal political parties to maintain ideological unity. Congress exemplifies the incapability of dealing with so many different foundations for politics as a single entity. The United States over-expanded geographically as a country and now, with the amount of population growth in each region and the strengthening of regional ethos, its federal system can't function as it was designed to do. The only way to reconcile this system without changing it is to give more autonomy to an executive power to decide matters with less consent from those being governed in order to break through gridlock, which is contrary to the founding values and beliefs of the United States.

Right now, the United States is living through arguably the most polarized period in American politics since the Civil War. And as long as the two-party federal system reigns on in its current form, Americans across the country will continue to suffer the negative effects, to the point that one day, the country's legislature literally will be incapable of debating and solving the biggest issues that face the country. No amount of biannual federal elections will solve that problem. The two-party system will continue to perpetuate. This means we, as Cascadians, will never be truly represented.

The only way a third party can become stable on the federal level in the United States is if it manages to capitalize on unclaimed political territory within a certain region, exploit the voting model used to elect candidates to federal positions in that region, and emphasize the issues to that specific region. As you can probably see, we have encountered a paradox. A stable and effective multi-minority party system across the country on a federal level requires the national ideological foundation that the United States does not possess. Therefore, any stable third party must exist to counteract the federal system, not work coherently with it. Third parties can't become stable with the population of the United States across the country. Any future third party that ends up remaining stable in influence and numbers[ix] will be due to its dominance in one specific region. And even then, since such a scenario would happen with a divergent region of lesser-influence, the significant impact such a party would make federally for the region it represents would still be inadequate to force the federal system to meet the needs of that region. In our case, Cascadians could bind together to form a Cascadian party, but the influence of this party would never amount to the numbers required to exert the level of influence needed in Washington, DC, to secure the level of freedom we deserve.

Even if the United States did manage to somehow change its system of representation to allow a greater number of political parties to succeed, it's no guarantee Cascadia would be any better off. North of the 49th parallel, the Canadian federal system has three major federal parties: the Conservative Party, the New Democratic Party, and the Liberal Party. Naturally, with three major parties

---

ix   Referring to representation in Congress.

representing the citizens of Canada on the federal level, the exchange of ideas is more diverse, and one could make a clear argument that political polarization is not as strong or hypersensitive as it is in the United States. But while the issues with the Canadian system of governance do not encompass the limiting of political representation, it does experience the effects of a splintered ideological foundation from a federal perspective. Canada has multiple distinct bioregions like the United States does. Each distinct region in Canada has its own unique foundation for identity, just as its American counterparts. The effects of bioregionalism aren't causing the same level of incoherency and gridlock as exists in Washington, DC, but they are beginning to wreak havoc on the divergent region of Cascadia that lies furthest west of Ottawa.

As you may recall when analyzing the Venn diagram example earlier in this chapter, the most practical option a democratic country's governing system has when dealing with a region whose ethos is too divergent from the collective whole is to force some amount of compliance or coherence onto said region. The Canadian federal government has endorsed and is attempting to force construction of a tar sands oil pipeline, known as the Enbridge Northern Gateway Pipeline, through the province of British Columbia, even though the local BC government has officially opposed this action. The Canadian government and its supporters says this pipeline will help safeguard Canada's economic future, while the pipeline's opponents argue it's a severe environmental hazard that risks permanent damage to the regional environment and that it tramples on the liberties of First Nations who hold legal rights to some of the land on which the pipeline will be built. This is, in my opinion, the most blatant example in current events that is evidence of Cascadia's divergence from the rest of the country. Furthermore, it is evidence of the fact that the current federal system has begun to work against our interests as Cascadians.

The fact that Canada has more diverse political representation in Ottawa isn't stopping this from happening. Cascadia's interests are still at risk. And yes, the minority parties vying to win the next election are vowing to overturn this effort by the Conservative Party's government.[x] But how long before these other parties, such as the Liberals and the New Democrats, turn an about-face on their current rhetoric and decide the pipeline is a good idea for Canada's economy after all? Surely once Canada starts suffering some negative effects economically, as its economic system operates under the same consumption-based model the United States does, more and more people outside Cascadia may grow to favor this project. The political leaders will have little choice but to support this course of action, lest they risk being voted out of office. The only option left then for Cascadia, if we wish to work with our current federal systems, is to try to strengthen regional representation, become more influential in Ottawa than we currently are, and attempt to force the other regions to comply more with us, to whatever extent is possible.

x   At the time this was written, the Conservative Party of Canada held a majority government.

This is what Quebec has done to some great effect in the last few decades. Quebec links its unique nationhood with its French foundations; these influences are vital to recognizing Quebec almost as a separate region within Canada. Quebec's unique historical background—being a predominantly French Canadian province with its own history and language remaining very prominent—also plays a part in keeping Canada's federal political focus in the eastern half of the country. While some Canadians might consider Quebec "divergent" from the Canadian norm, Quebec has always played a central role in helping define the Canadian identity. Furthermore, apart from its auxiliary characteristics (e.g., language, cultural history, French influence) that differentiate it from the rest of Laurentia—the bioregion most of Quebec's population lives in—Quebec very much shares the same natural ethos as that of its neighboring provinces (i.e., Ontario, New Brunswick) and states (i.e., Vermont, upstate New York). The ways to live in these places and thrive are very similar when analyzing the structure of economy and the bases of human interaction. Nevertheless, Quebec's distinct history, which has set it apart from other provinces since before Canada became a confederation, plays a significant enough impact in its identity. Thusly, Quebec is officially considered its own nation inside the country of Canada, even though it lacks unique ecological factors.

Quebec also has a strong history of shaping federal politics in Canada. For most of the latter half of the twentieth century and up until 2011, no prime minister of Canada to lead a majority government came from outside of Quebec. Its politicians have also used this influence to curtail legislation in Quebec's favor, often to the contempt of other provinces in Canada. The Bloc Quebecois is the federal political party representing solely the interests of Quebec; its presence in Parliament for much of recent history has led to what many in Canada consider the over-representation of Quebec in federal politics. Many claim it has wielded undue influence over discourse and legislation, effectively forcing the other regions to comply with its will. In the early to mid-1990s, the supporters of the Bloc Quebecois nearly had enough votes to secure secession. The 1995 referendum acquired 49.4% in favor of Quebec's independence. In order to keep Quebec as a prominent province in Canada instead of becoming its own country, many political concessions have been made to Quebec to appease its citizens.

Some in Cascadia may look to the Bloc as an example of how Cascadians should proceed politically. A few factors, however, would prohibit a similar Cascadian political party from achieving any kind of similar success as the Bloc has had in recent decades. First, Cascadia exists in two countries, whereas Quebec exists only in one. Furthermore, Quebec is its own province—a unified political entity—whereas Cascadia is split among several different states and a province. The likelihood a Cascadian political party could work effectively across multiple states and a province and across international borders is questionable at best. Too many factors challenge the practicality of a unified, regionalist political party existing in two countries, not to mention the fact that such a

regionalist party is unlikely to make any sort of significant headway in the United States' political system for
the reasons I've already outlined.

Second, Cascadia has an identity divergent from the
United States and Canada, whereas Quebec has always
played a central role in shaping the identity of Canada as
a whole. This is why Quebec is still considered very much
"Canadian" in character, even though it has a different ethnic foundation, and its people use a different language.
Quebec's ethos, on the most fundamental level, is very
much synced with the dominant Laurentian ethos that encompasses a majority of the Canadian population. This is a
very significant reason why Quebec has been able—and is
still able—to be sufficiently represented in the Canadian
federal system.[xi] Cascadia's ethos is not synced with the
dominant influences in either of our two countries. At best,
our ability to sway federal policies in our favor in either
country would be severely handicapped. The rest of our
countries' populations—a large majority of Americans and
Canadians—would have little incentive to accommodate
our will in the current federal systems.

Third, the Bloc is seen as a one-sided political party; its platform contains numerous references to social
democratic ideology[73], and it's largely identified as left of

---

xi   While the Bloc Quebecois lost nearly all of its seats in parliament in the 2011 Canadian federal elections, 57% of the seats
won by the New Democratic Party, which became the official opposition after these elections, came from Quebec. Furthermore,
Quebec MP Thomas Mulcair became leader of the opposition
following the passing of Jack Layton.

center. It has been able to acquire a significant number of votes from more conservative areas in Quebec, most notably in the 1993 elections, when the Bloc became the official opposition party in Canadian Parliament, but that ability has diminished in recent years. The Bloc even has trouble maintaining majority influence in Quebec, as evidenced by the 2011 general elections when it lost nearly all of its seats in Parliament. To that point, nearly all of the seats lost by the Bloc in that election were won by the New Democratic Party, a left-of-center, social democratic party. How many votes does the Bloc lose by not espousing a more inclusive political ideology? How many proud Quebecois, possibly sympathetic to the possibility of independence, vote for another federal party because they don't feel properly represented by the Bloc? By focusing regional representation into a political party—local or federal—you run a huge risk of alienating those in the region who hold a personal political ideology different from what a regional party's platform or votes indicate. Creating a political party that is inclusive to the point of incorporating an entire regional spectrum of political ideologies may be possible, but it is not the most viable. A party's job is often to vote as one united front so it maintains influence. If a Cascadian political party were created and voted on issues with a manner consistent with just one ideology, such as social democratic or libertarian, it would risk alienating all other proud Cascadians who don't hold that same political ideology.

Our federal systems are not designed to properly represent us as Cascadians. In the United States, it's nearly impossible to have a regionalist party in Congress, and any attempt at solidifying a permanent third party has not been successful in post-Civil War history. In Canada, regionalist parties can be viable, but they only maintain their viability as long as their ethos and strength in numbers remain central to the country's identity. The Cascadian ethos is not central to the federal identities of Canada or the United States; we're divergent from the norm. This means that Cascadians cannot succeed in achieving the representation and influence needed to bring our regional society back into balance in either country. This conclusion brings us to the next rational question: can we fundamentally change our current federal systems so we, as Cascadians, can be allowed to thrive? Or to ask this question from another perspective, can American or Canadians come together, within our respective countries, and agree on fundamental reform to our federal systems of governance and representation so that we, as Cascadians, can secure the liberties needed, so we can bring our regional society back into balance as we see fit?

Such fundamental reform would require changes to constitutional principles. If we go back to the metaphor of a team playing the game, this is the scenario where all team members would need to agree on some very significant rule changes, with the goal of improving the functionality of each individual and, thus, the team as whole. If all team members are unified in identity and purpose, then such a scenario is definitely plausible. Each individual, although fundamentally different from one another, has enough commonality to find compromise and agree on significant changes for the good of each other and the whole team. However, when we apply this metaphor to our regionalist reality as countries, we remember that the Cascadian ethos—our identity, our foundational principles, our driving values, and our story—is not the same as the rest of the continent. We are the divergent region that is becoming more apparent as each day passes. Fundamental changes to our federal system may technically be possible according to our respective constitutional principles, but the effects of bioregionalism and Cascadian divergence will make any change agreed upon by our respective countries insufficient for our region and our freedom. To that point—my second reason for why it is impractical for us to work within our current federal systems—there are a couple of issues to address. One is that any fundamental change to the federal systems of representation and governance is highly unlikely to occur in our current time in the United States or Canada. And another is that any fundamental change to these federal systems of representation agreed upon by either country likely will not benefit Cascadia.

In the United States, such a change would require a constitutional amendment, a process that requires the consent of two-thirds of both the United States House of Representatives and the United States Senate, in addition to the consent of three-fourths of the states in the Union through their respective legislative bodies. The last time this process was completed successfully, with regard to a proposal being both submitted and ratified within a finite time span of four years or less,[xii] was 1971 when the Twenty-Sixth Amendment was adopted, denying the prohibition of voting rights for anyone at least eighteen years of age. In Canada, amending the constitution, which is made up of several legal documents and codes instead of just one, as in the United States, requires a resolution to be passed by both the House of Commons and the Senate, in addition to the consent of seven provinces that represent at least half of the country's population through their provincial legislative bodies. Since the adoption of the Constitution Act of 1982, there have been eleven constitutional amendments adopted in Canada.

It is certainly possible for a constitutional amendment to be submitted and ratified in similar manners today in either country, but bioregionalism now has a more significant effect on this process than it ever had before. When it comes to an issue as significant as how people should be represented in government, each region will have a different political foundation from which to address that question. Furthermore, each other region may have something to lose in terms of political influence, should an amendment securing adequate representation of Cascadians ever be adopted. It is Cascadia's divergent identity that will be accommodated in such a scenario, forcing the other regions to give up some aspects of their own representation, with which they likely will not be comfortable. If anything, the only change that would be

---

xii   The 27th Amendment was adopted in 1992, but it was originally submitted in 1789, along with the original ten amendments that became known as the Bill of Rights.

agreeable to the number of states or provinces needed to adopt an amendment would be one that attempts to force Cascadia to become less divergent. This, of course, would be blatantly detrimental to our region. Passing one amendment is hard enough; passing one that fundamentally alters how people are represented and secures true freedom for Cascadians is all but impossible. This may be good for the stability of our countries' political institutions, but it proves to be an obstacle to solving fundamental issues that go to the core of our political foundation as Cascadians.

This brings us to my third and final reason why it is impractical for Cascadia to truly thrive and be free within our current federal systems. Even if we could, hypothetically speaking, achieve the fundamental changes needed in the United States and Canada, we would still be a nation split between two different countries. Our attempts to cooperate together as one region across international borders are already hindered by federal laws and would continue to be so, even under more optimal legal conditions. No matter how much political or legal power could be transferred to the Cascadian region from Ottawa or Washington, DC, no state, province, or region can act unilaterally to create political or legal arrangements across an international border. Such power belongs, rightfully, at the federal level. No state, province, or region within a country should have the power to undermine the rest of the country by agreeing to anything that could cause its respective union harm. These types of arrangements need to be conducted on federal levels with respect to precedence and international law. Our potential as Cascadians to maximize our interdependence and to create economic opportunities is ripe if we were to look at our status quo from a regional perspective. But such potential is and would continue to be exerted through a federal model where the interests and forces of regions outside of Cascadia take hold in any deal or agreement struck between the United States and Canadian governments. As has happened before and will happen again, economic opportunities are realized for our two countries, but at a cost to Cascadia as a region. Our potential in Cascadia is permanently restrained because of an arbitrary border that becomes less and less sensible to us each day. We, as a region, are unified through environment and ethos. This is a fact—a reality of ecologic and geographic condition. No amount of fundamental change or devolution of political power within the United States and Canada will change this and satisfy our potential as Cascadians.

We don't respond to the root causes of our problems as Americans and Canadians, addressing the fundamental differences in our identities and value systems, because neither of our countries has a united voice to do so. And as we continue to try to find ways of "national reconciliation" within either of our countries, we fail to step back and see the big picture—our current federal statuses quo in the United States and Canada are not cohesive paintings of a single style or method but a diverse canvas with several distinct parts fundamentally disconnected from one another. This brings us to the only rational question left to ask: if we can't fix our current federal systems to bring Cascadia back into balance, what can we do?

Our affinity towards the United States and Canada, including the pride we feel for our respective countries, need not be destroyed. There's still so much good and hope within the values we recognize as American and Canadian that we don't need to replace. What needs to be replaced is the subconscious link these ideas have with the federal institutions of power in Ottawa and Washington, DC. This is the first step in the process of accepting what must be done. It is not the White House, or Capitol Hill, or Parliament Hill that gives us our sense of freedom in Cascadia; it's the grandeur of the region we call home. Supporting the values of freedom, service, and pride we share as Cascadians, regardless of our personal political beliefs, is something we can do by acknowledging Cascadia and without hostility or ill will towards the United States or Canada.

Unlike most other democratic countries around the planet, our democracies and political boundaries are not forged by long-standing traditions, ethnic barriers, or strict cultural adherences. The United States and Canada are two countries built upon a foundation of multinationalism and multiculturalism. And unlike most other nations, we in Cascadia can use this to our advantage. Not only can we coexist peacefully as individuals despite the innate differences in our characteristics, but we also can learn from each other's beliefs and teachings to advance as one society and as one region more capably than any other region on the planet. We're on a unique continent in a unique situation with a very unique opportunity to permanently move beyond the critical obstacles that inhibit our progress as a region *without* destroying the integrity of either the United States or Canada. It is true that we cannot go back to how things used to be. Our experiences and our shared history have shaped the existence of our two countries, and nothing can change that reality. As we as people must do to survive, our countries must learn from our past, analyze our present, and evolve for the sake of our future.

The United States and Canada will have a choice to make. We, as citizens of one or both of our two countries, must choose whether we are countries of free people or empires—we cannot, by nature, be both. When a country overexpands geographically, it runs the risk dominating the naturally influenced ethos that is too divergent from the other(s) within it. When that happens, a country can no longer be considered as one of free people who work cohesively together; rather, it is an empire where the will of the dominant triumphs over the others within its own borders. Resources are utilized from each region to benefit that same will. The United States and Canada overexpanded geographically long ago, and they risked subjugating the communities of Cascadia, both native and those established from its settlers, once that happened. Now, our Cascadian ethos is being metaphorically pushed around and violated by the others. We unquestionably need a fundamental change to our status quo and our political foundations. A day will come when change is inevitable, and we will have a choice—we can give in to fear of the unknown and seal our fate in an ambiance of instability, or we can overcome fear of the unknown by opening the door to new possibilities.

6. THE PROSPECT OF CASCADIAN INDEPENDENCE

We are not powerless, hopeless beings who can do nothing but wait for the worst to come. We are remarkable, intelligent people who will and should own our future. Our continent is on a collision course with harsh reality—we simply do not have enough natural resources for the most fortunate societies to continue consuming at current rates. If everyone lived the lifestyle of an average American citizen, taking into consideration what and how much resources one consumes on an average day, we would need the equivalent of five planet Earths' worth of natural resources in order to sustain this.[74] If we choose not to take control over our own future as Cascadians and take the steps towards incorporating more sustainable, locally based ways of life, we risk living through rapid economic and social deterioration. The result of this reality would be devastating poverty, unemployment, and even more limited influence over the democratic systems of governance that are supposed to work for us. The aftermath of whatever order can be sustained following this period of instability would be true dystopia—a nightmare of circumstance that nobody deserves.

I refuse to believe we cannot or should not do anything in the face of such a dire inevitability. We do not need to wait for this happen. We can make fundamental changes to our society to curb this course of events into something manageable and something desirable. We, as individuals and communities, can do so much right now in the aspect of our daily lives to make positive, fundamental changes to how we live. Many of us have already begun making such changes and have even inspired community-based initiatives to live more sustainably. This is just the beginning; these small changes by individuals and communities in our region are propagating into a greater movement of consciousness. We should and will progress towards a better future that we safeguard and do right by. What has begun in the realms of local economics and local culture will conclude in a new political reality for our region. We are Cascadia; all we need to do is acknowledge its possibility and work for this new reality as one united region.

I refer, of course, to the actualization of bioregionalism in our daily lives and the culmination of a new country in our relative immediate future. If we were to narrow down the scope of this vision into a tangible goal, it would read as such:

Create a sociopolitical movement that unites an irrefutable majority of people in a vast region/nation of the continent and convinces them to embark upon a new journey of realizing freedom by recognizing our bioregional reality, and create a new country out of the two that already exist.

It sounds like a task beyond daunting, perhaps even unattainable. But I believe wholeheartedly that it's anything but that. The process has already begun; achieving the goal of this vision is simply a matter of when. This is not utopian or impossible; if anything, blindly continuing along our current trajectory towards societal catastrophe, assuming everything will be fine and that the status quo will work itself out is hopelessly utopian dogma. Unrestrained economic growth, sustained by the world's developed countries and pursued relentlessly by those still developing, will lead to a breaking point in the near future as the earth does not possess the amount of resources needed to maintain the material affluence desired or expected under this consumerist-based paradigm. Proceeding in this over-consumptive manner will lead to global economic collapse.[75] Simply put, the status quo cannot continue. The vision for Cascadia—the aspects of our daily lives that will fundamentally change, as well as the achievement of a new country—is sensible and pragmatic.

In this chapter, I will propose a practical, legal path forward to tangibly achieve this vision. What I propose has not been done before, but that does not mean it's illegitimate or impractical. My hope is that after reading about this proposal and its reasoning, even the most skeptical or those adamantly against the idea of secession—as I was, not long before beginning my research for this book—will thoughtfully consider a brand new possibility that they will consider legitimate, regardless of whether those feelings change any time soon.

When talking about the prospects for Cascadia, it's very easy to get wrapped up in the political reality. What would a Cascadian government look like? What would be included in a Cascadian Constitution? What would a bioregional reality specifically entail in areas of public policy? I do not have the answers to these questions, nor should I. These answers will come in time, through greater public discourse. And this discourse will be a by-product, not the main focus, of a powerful awareness movement that unites the people of this region under the Cascadian ethos. My focus is on proving, to the best of my ability, an innovative idea to achieve a brand new status quo, should we choose to work for it. There are, after all, numerous options when it comes to choosing an actual system of governance that would allow us to enable a bioregional reality. Some of us may favor a system that resembles Western federal democracies. Some of us may favor a system that radically shifts away from a statist model. Perhaps some of us will favor some sort of hybrid system that hasn't been fully thought of yet.

When the time comes for us to seriously consider tangible alternatives, we'll come together as one united people and reach a conclusion. To focus on the question of which exact system we should favor at this time is putting the cart a mile ahead of the horse, so to speak. The important things to keep in mind now, while our movement is still young, are the factors in any potential system that would allow us to truly thrive as Cascadians.

I would like to emphasize, however, that we must be cautious about pursuing an alternative that is too radically different from our familiarity. Bioregional-ism naturally favors devolution of public power away from a centralized state, but this does not necessarily mean, for instance, that a federal institution is completely incompatible. Consider a system in which no mechanism for regional unity exists. Such a radically devolved vision across an entire society could result in complete isolation and dysfunction in what should be a nation united. For any such idea so extreme to become reality in any realistic time frame for the relatively near future, drastic social change would need to happen in very short order. An impractical paradigm shift of how our society functions on the most basic levels would need to not only occur but be embraced by a vast majority within that society. Even the most progressive minds have the inclination to reject such drastic change if the situation does not warrant it for means of survival. For such an elemental shift to occur in this scenario, the basis for society we know today would need to be become irreversibly unstable. This would likely happen under the duress of a total economic collapse, prolonged and severe natural events of destruction, or violent conflict instigated by fear or unrest. And as we've witnessed countless times in modern history, people tend to gravitate towards tradition and social order, which in our case would be the opposite of bioregionalism, when faced with such catastrophic changes in society.

These are not scenarios I wish to see occur or live through, even if it meant a more ideal end result after the turmoil subsided. No cultural movement is worth mass suffering or the loss of life, if it can be avoided. We must look beyond the prospect of surviving the inevitable collapse of an imperialistic society; we must work proactively to change our present condition for the sake of progress so badly needed. And if that means we embrace some aspects of constitutionality, governance, or politics with which we are currently familiar in order to make necessary fundamental changes to our status quo, then it may very well be prudent to do so instead of accepting nothing less than an absolutist notion.

A free, united, sovereign Cascadia—this is the goal within the political sphere of influence. The legitimacy of Cascadia's self-determination is within us and not inherent in our current political systems. Our identity and our freedom are not inherent in the American or Canadian federal states or in the constitutional documents that are meant to safeguard them. Our identity and our freedom wouldn't even be inherent in a Cascadian state or any similar institution; that's simply one of the most optimal mechanisms to secure these intangibles in our current time. Our identity and our freedom come from this awesome and profound region, its natural essence, and the higher power that created it. But until we truly unite and free this region in the political sense, Cascadia will always be subservient to the will of regions to our east. Should we choose to work for independence, we must work within our current systems of governance, utilizing existing mechanisms present in our democratic institutions, to enact the change we wish to see. In order to achieve the legitimate sovereignty and unity we desire, without a complete collapse of our current societies, we must act accordingly with the current federal systems and constitutional principles seen as legitimate. With a united vision and proactive action, we will make progress within the political realm to achieve Cascadian independence. The question we need to answer now is, when the time comes for independence, how do we forge a regional movement into an independent nation?

Before I go into detail, I cannot stress enough the importance that what follows will be only the result of the organic growth of a much broader social movement. Working within our political reality and trying to answer questions of political legitimacy is important; hence, I will outline a practical path forward within this sphere of influence. But there is so much we can and should do outside of the realm of politics to help achieve the Cascadian future we desire. Right now, we, as individuals and organizations, can network and work together as a region. We can build awareness of Cascadia and Cascadian identity, as well as realizing our regional potential, without entering the formal political arena. We can act locally and interact on a regional level in areas of business, education, innovation, conservation, and more. We can invest in new energy technologies. We can begin teaching ourselves and our children about the history of this region. We can curb the behavior of corporations that operate here by choosing what we buy and what we endorse. We can do all of this and more, which is what groups like the CascadiaNow![i] are working on. There will be a time to devote attention to politics; that time will come on its own accord when we, as a region, are more ready to do so. The most important thing we can focus on right now—the one thing that will support subsequent efforts to achieve our vision—is to unite all in this region under a single Cascadian identity: the Cascadian ethos. In this sense, while this movement will eventually work to change our civic and political status quo, the focus on culture and ways of life is far more essential to ensuring that any permanent change made to our civic and political status quo actually will last. The Cascadia movement should and will center on areas of culture and lifestyle, first and foremost, in the immediate future; Cascadian bioregionalism needs to be understood in these terms first before it can be expanded upon to create a new political reality. "Cascadian" must become just as much of a prominent nonpolitical identity as are "American" and "Canadian."

Most are aware that living in the Pacific Northwest is different from living in other places, but few are aware of what makes us unique—why our value systems and culture are similar throughout the entire region, regardless of political differences, and how we're bound together as a common people, regardless of our intrinsic or social differences. These concepts must be understood and embraced in order for Cascadia, as we envision it, to become reality. If the individuals in this region do not embrace

---

i   http://www.cascadianow.org

the Cascadian ethos and do not identify as Cascadian, then no movement towards a new political reality can grow organically from that. We must outreach and bring together American and Canadian, urban and rural, progressive and libertarian, native and immigrant, religious and atheist—everyone in and throughout this region to be realized as one. We have an enormous opportunity to hone this identity for the younger generations growing up now and fill the rapidly growing void of fulfillment from our current federal identities. The issues and values that our young people take to heart in this region are constantly ignored or re-framed to benefit the powerful in Washington, D.C. and Ottawa; we can help make Cascadia their vision too. Most throughout this region must truly feel Cascadian first and foremost; "Cascadian" must become our primary national identity. Eventually, being American or Canadian will become an identity of circumstance. There is no need to belittle, chastise, or attack the American and Canadian national identities; we must simply work to make our regional ethos the greater influence of those who reside here.

The sociopolitical Cascadian movement, in its broad sense, will encompass many facets of our daily lives in this region, from politics to economics, from sports to media, and everything in between. I cannot predict everything that will be a part of the movement, but I know the movement will have four main characteristics, if it is to succeed. First, the movement will have one singular goal that individuals and organizations that consider themselves part of it will work towards: self-determination.

This goal is the destination in our journey that is currently just beginning. It is also a goal that can be adapted by anyone, regardless of who that person is and what specifics he or she desires. The singularity and simplicity of this goal is vital. If this movement becomes about more than self-determination—such as self-determination *and* alternative energy production, or self-determination *and* the right to consume marijuana, or self-determination *and* a decentralized governmental structure—it will become exclusionary beyond the natural point of geography and bioregional principles. The movement will subsequently fracture and diminish because certain sects of it will become too focused on ideology.

Second, the movement will not be based in ideology or focused on the exclusion of others. It will be based on affirming the reality of our regional ethos and including everyone in this region. Radical acceptance of different viewpoints will be needed in order for this movement to grow and succeed with one single goal being the driving force. Even if someone does not realize it yet, anyone living in this region has the potential to embody the Cascadian ethos and identify as Cascadian, through and through. A movement that tries to promote only a "certain type" of Cascadian or exclude those who "aren't Cascadian enough" will maintain division in this region and play favor to the status quo.

Third, the movement will not be based in fear of our political and financial instabilities. It will be based in optimism for the possibilities of our Cascadian vision. Any movement that uses fear as the motivation for support fails when that which fear is directed toward begins to subside. Once the status quo changes slightly, causing relief, there's less of a need to be afraid and, thus, less of a need to support such a movement based on that fear. A strong and successful movement must be based in a hopeful vision in which support for it does not wane with slight changes in the status quo.

Fourth and finally, the movement will not be reactionary in nature; it will be proactive in nature. Reactionary emotions tend to be intense but are not sustainable for long periods. Any movement based in anger in reaction to the status quo will fizzle out in short order once that status quo returns to a more comfortable state. A proactive movement, focused on opportunities and progress that could be made to change the status quo can be sustained until the goal of the movement is attained. Orientation around a single goal, affirmation, optimism, and proactivity—these are the qualities of which the broad Cascadian movement and everything that will constitute it will be made.

Now, pertaining to how to achieve independence, let's start with what we know will *not* work. The respective Supreme Courts in both the United States and Canada have resolved that unilateral secession—the act of a state or province to secede from its respective union by its own volition—is unlawful and unconstitutional. The United States fought a bloody civil war, in part, due to this issue. Whether or not you agree with the legal foundations for these decisions, they are the laws of our lands. So I say with the utmost conviction: we must not revolt—nor do we need to. Secession without the consent of our fellow citizens in the United States and Canada, otherwise known as unilateral secession, is not an option. *Period.*

As the Confederacy learned during the American Civil War, the reality of attempting to secede unilaterally is devastating—and would be again. Our movement would be demonized by our neighbors and fellow citizens. Conflict and violence would likely spill over into the streets of our towns and cities. We would be branded as radicals and terrorists—enemies of freedom and peace. Trade and financial assistance to our communities would be swiftly cut. All but the most delusional, hardcore believers would abandon the movement. We would receive worldwide condemnation from members of the international community with which we aspire to be friendly. Any possibility for a united, free Cascadia of our dreams would be postponed for generations. Attempted revolution is not warranted and would only end in absolute disaster. The United States and Canada are inefficient and convoluted federal systems, but they are not tyrannical regimes. Any sober-minded individual can recognize this. When we speak out against our elected officials, we are not hunted down by police to be imprisoned or executed. Our family members are not kidnapped or murdered for disagreeing with the status quo. We are not forced to live our lives according to the expectations of an oligarchy or an autocracy. We may disagree with certain legal statutes and certain actions committed by the United States and/ or Canadian federal governments, but we have a judicial

system and democratic processes to address our griev-
ances.

If freedom was an absolute state, where it either
existed or it didn't, then it would be easy to argue that
revolt is necessary. But as I proposed earlier in this book,
freedom is a balance of liberties that continually changes
and fluctuates through the course of events; it's a state in
flux, conditional, and one that exists in varying degrees.
I argue that the legal and political statuses quo in the
United States and Canada, while not perfect to any one
individual, does not constitute a reality that suppresses
our freedom, as Cascadians, to a point where revolution
could be considered a viable or ethical option. Until we
reach such a point, when federal officers are jailing or ex-
ecuting people for simply speaking their minds, or when
our federal institutions of power strip certain rights of
certain people in an attempt to gain obedience, or when
our federal institutions of power sit idly by with passive
approval while private firms forcibly take unwarranted actions against us, we have no rational justification for trying
to revolt against either the United States or Canada. I do
not foresee such a time ever occurring, and I pray that it
never does. Our goal is not to overthrow the United States
and/or Canadian governments; our goal is to separate ourselves and coexist peacefully alongside them. Nonviolence
is absolutely pivotal—I argue, fundamental—in our efforts
towards achieving Cascadian independence. We must
never reach a point where we feel the need to engage in
violent conflict, reactionary or otherwise, to literally fight
for a new future under circumstances that are less than

extreme. We must be willing to look beyond even the most intense adversity and confront the fear and prejudices of others with a calm, rational demeanor. This is how we will win over the hearts and minds of those who are hesitant to support our cause, both in and outside of the Cascadian region. Nonviolence will prevail for us, just as it has for countless other movements in recent history around the world. It is our only viable option moving forward. The days of "glorious revolutions" and shooting our way to freedom are over. It will not take brute force to achieve a new political reality. We live in an enlightened twenty-first-century Western democracy, and we will conduct our movement accordingly.

As I alluded to earlier, there is a lawful, constitutional path forward to achieve independence in both the United States and Canada—secession with the consent of our respective federal unions, otherwise known as consented release. I argue it is this legal mechanism we should utilize as one united region in both the United States and Canada to achieve independence. To do this successfully, it will require the following:

- A clearly defined alternative to the current federal institutions of power

- An irrefutable amount of political capital among the general populous of Cascadia

- A moral argument for secession's justification that wins support from those outside Cascadia

The first two items are essential to moving forward with the legal processes for secession in both countries, while the third item is vital to the final pivotal step in the legal process in gaining consent from both federal institutions.

Pertaining to the first two items, political capital— popular support for the idea of Cascadia among those in our region—is just beginning to be acquired. The increased awareness, discussion, and visual presence of Cascadian ideas in the public, social sphere of influence are evidence of this. This is the current primary goal of the Cascadian movement. There will come a time, after the movement has influenced most throughout the region, where the idea of Cascadia and support for self-determination reaches critical mass. Getting to this point will require a lot of dedication, hard work, and patience by those who support Cascadia, but it will come in due time. It is at this point where we, as a region, should come together to define and propose a clear alternative and path forward seen as legitimate. I'm referring to assets such as a constitutional convention, a proposed constitutional document, a legal road map, and the like. These assets need the input of all those who support Cascadia when the level of support is sufficient to warrant them. Trying to create these assets in our present day, when support for Cascadia is still relatively small, is irrational. Once they are settled on, though, through mediums of public discourse, we will possess the legal foundations for which to operate under a legitimate alternative to the status quo.

It is at this point where we may need a grand, unified statement that clearly shows irrefutable support for this clear alternative. There are different ways to do this, such as a declaration endorsed by our respective local representative bodies (e.g., state legislatures, provincial parliament) or a region-wide, nonbinding referendum. This statement would be the measurement of support that those in and outside of Cascadia use as justification for popular sovereignty. If we were to assign a number to it, such as a percentage of Cascadians needed to achieve the level of support that could legitimately be considered as "irrefutable," I would propose a number around 60%. After all, secession is not something you attempt to move forward with a bare majority of 50.1%. If a presidential candidate wins 60% of the popular vote in a general election, he or she likely wins nearly every single state in the Union. If a political party wins 60% of the popular vote for the House of Representatives, it will likely acquire at least three hundred seats and a mandate to dominate the legislative agenda. If a political party wins 60% of the popular vote for Parliament, it will likely win nearly every seat in the House of Commons. 60% (or a percentage thereabout) is an appropriate percentage, which clearly demonstrates an irrefutable majority in a free, democratic society.

Just as important as the measured level of support, though, is how wide-reaching this majority is. If majority support is one-sided and exclusive, it will never reach the level needed in Cascadia to be truly irrefutable. Irrefutable political capital must be acquired from just about every demographic segment that exists: men; women; left-of-center voters; right-of-center voters; unaffiliated moderate voters; religious people; atheists; people in cities, suburbs, and rural areas; natives; immigrants; people of many different ethnic and racial backgrounds; people with different sexual orientations; people with different gender identities; people of different ages; and people from every municipality and ecoregion across Cascadia. Once this is achieved, we'll have a clear alternative in the foundations for a Cascadian country and overwhelming, irrefutable support, both seen as legitimate by those involved in this process. The legally-binding procedures to secure independence can then commence.

Because each country has its own process of seceding legally and constitutionally, I will cover them one country at a time to avoid confusion. It should be understood, however, that these procedures should coincide with each other and happen within the same time frame. First, let me begin with the United States of America. The only time it has ever dealt with the experiment of secession was in the 1860s, when a number of states claimed unilateral rights to secede from the Union and formed the self-identified Confederate States of America. The position taken by the United States and President Abraham Lincoln was not that secession in itself was illegal but that seceding without the consent acquired from states assembled in Congress was illegal, and the Confederacy was therefore illegitimate. President Lincoln clearly demonstrates this in his first inaugural address:

> I hold that, in contemplation of universal law, and
> of the Constitution, the union of these States is

perpetual....It follows....that no State, *upon its own mere motion*, can lawfully get out of the Union; that resolves and ordinances to that effect are legally void . . . I, therefore, consider that, in view of the Constitution and the laws, the Union is unbroken."[76] (emphasis mine)

The states that formed the Confederate States of America disagreed with the notion that unilateral secession was unlawful and attempted to do so anyway. This led to a very contentious and violent civil war in which hundreds of thousands of people were killed.

After the war ended, a case before the Supreme Court known as Texas v. White—regarding the sale of US treasury bonds by the state of Texas after it had attempted to secede and joined the Confederacy—addressed the constitutionality of secession. In the majority decision, Chief Justice Samuel Chase wrote the following:

The Union of the States never was a purely artificial and arbitrary relation. It began among the Colonies, and grew out of common origin, mutual sympathies, kindred principles, similar interests, and geographical relations. It was confirmed and strengthened by the necessities of war, and received definite form and character and sanction from the Articles of Confederation. By these, *the Union was solemnly declared to 'be perpetual.'* And when these Articles were found to be inadequate to the exigencies of the country, the Constitution was ordained 'to form a more perfect Union.' It is difficult to convey the idea of indissoluble unity more clearly than by these words. *What can be indissoluble if a perpetual Union, made more perfect, is not?*

But the perpetuity and indissolubility of the Union by no means implies the loss of distinct and individual existence, or of the right of self-government, by the States. Under the Articles of Confederation, each State retained its sovereignty, freedom, and independence, and every power, jurisdiction, and right not expressly delegated to the United States. Under the Constitution, though the powers of the States were much restricted, still all powers not delegated to the United States nor prohibited to the States, are reserved to the States respectively, or to the people. And we have already had occasion to remark at this term that:

The people of each State compose a State, having its own government, and endowed with all the functions essential to separate and independent existence;'

And that, 'without the States in union, there could be no such political body as the United States.' *Not only, therefore, can there be no loss of separate and independent autonomy to the States through their union under the Constitution, but it may be not unreasonably said that the preservation of the States, and the maintenance of their governments, are as much within the design and care of the Constitution*

*as the preservation of the Union and the mainte-
nance of the National government.* The Constitution, in all its provisions, looks to an indestructible
Union composed of indestructible States.

When, therefore, Texas became one of the United
States, she entered into an indissoluble relation.
All the obligations of perpetual union, and all the
guaranties of republican government in the Union,
attached at once to the State. *The act which con-
summated her admission into the Union was something more than a compact; it was the incorporation
of a new member into the political body. And it was
final.*[77] (emphasis mine)

This set the precedent that, because the Union was
designed to be perpetual and indestructible, it is necessary and essential to maintain states as part of the Union.
No state, unto itself, is allowed to dissolve its admission
into the Union. This decision declared that Texas, and
all other states that claimed secession, never actually
seceded but instead remained in a position of insurrection throughout the war. This rationale justified the federal government's authority to take necessary action and
destroy the insurrection so that the states might once
again take their proper place in the Union. By reading
this excerpt, you might have concluded that secession is
not legal and not possible without revolution. However,
Chief Justice Chase had one more thing to say regarding
a state's membership status within the Union:

> The union between Texas and the other States was as complete, as perpetual, and as indissoluble as the union between the original States. There was no place for reconsideration or revocation, except through revolution or *through consent of the States.*[78] (emphasis mine)

This last statement, "except . . . through consent of the States," means that a vote of secession can be legal; it just has to be done through the states in question *and* Congress.

This language derives directly from Article IV, Section 3, of the Constitution of the United States, which pertains to the admittance of new states into the Union and the powers of Congress regarding this matter:

> New States may be admitted by the Congress into this Union; but no new State shall be formed or erected within the Jurisdiction of any other State; nor any State be formed by the Junction of two or more States, or Parts of States, *without the Consent of the Legislatures of the States concerned as well as of the Congress.*
>
> *The Congress shall have Power to dispose of and make all needful Rules and Regulations respecting the Territory or other Property belonging to the United States*; and nothing in this Constitution shall be so construed as to Prejudice any Claims of the United States, or of any particular State.[79] (emphasis mine)

Since Congress has the powers prescribed to admit a state into the Union by granting a territory the status of statehood, it stands to reason that Congress also has the power to grant a state the status of territory, as long as the state in question has consented to such change. And as is clearly stated in Article IV, Congress has the power to dispose of or release any territory within its jurisdiction. This is the constitutional mechanism that a state or group of states can use to be released from the Union, with the consent of states assembled in Congress.

Essentially, this means we would need to use Article IV, Section 3, in reverse. When this article is used as written, Congress grants territory statehood by a simple majority vote after said territory clearly demonstrates its desire to join the Union. Historically, this is done through a popular referendum and completes the requirements of its petition for statehood.[ii] To properly use this article in order to achieve the status of territory, so that Congress can properly dispose of said territory, a bill would need to be passed in each state legislature within the Cascadian region and signed by each governor, to designate the area of that state—part of the state or its entirety—which would become federal territory and subject to the jurisdiction of Congress. Each bill would either redraw the borders of that state, separating the area remaining a state within the Union and the area becoming federal territory, or designate the entire state to become federal territory, and, if necessary, declare its state government

ii   Creating a constitution that provides for a republican form of government.

dissolved. For example, a bill in the state of Washington would designate the entire state as federal territory—thus, its state government no longer would need to exist—while a bill in the state of Montana would designate the area agreed upon as Cascadian to become federal territory and redefine that state's western border. Furthermore, a bill, if applicable, would designate the part of the state remaining within the Union to become part of a neighboring state, subject to the neighboring state's acceptance through a similar bill. For example, a bill in the state of Oregon would designate a majority of the state to become federal territory and its state government dissolved but leaves a small portion of its land to the south to remain in the Union. This area would be of such low population that remaining an independent state would be impractical for the purposes of federal representation and would, therefore, be designated to become part of Nevada and/or California, should Nevada and/or California choose to accept. These bills would also compel but not force Congress to consent, in accordance with the will of the people of these states, and release the newly declared federal territory from congressional jurisdiction in order for it to unite and become part of the new country of Cascadia.

And last, these bills would expressly declare that the effects of its contents would not be actionable until Congress passed a bill to acknowledge and consent to the agreements reached by these states, thereby achieving consent of the states assembled through Congress.

Logistically, this means that the states of Idaho, Oregon, and Washington would each need to pass a bill that declared all or most of their geography to become Cascadian territory under the jurisdiction of Congress and the state governments dissolved. This also means that the states of Alaska, California, Montana, Nevada, Utah, and Wyoming would each need to pass a bill agreeing to new state borders, declaring the appropriate parts of its state as Cascadian territory and, if applicable, accepting the parts of another state being dissolved as part of its own state. Such a bill from each of these six states, in which a majority is not Cascadian, will likely require compensation in order to make it politically viable to its general populous. The moral justifications[iii] alone may not be enough to secure the passage of these bills. These considerations should be expected obstacles that can be planned for and met accordingly. Once these bills are passed and signed by each governor,[iv] the area to become Cascadia will be, in its entirety, federal territory upon acceptance and consent from Congress.

At this point, it will then be up to Congress to agree to consent to the state bills passed, thereby creating Cascadian territory, and to release said territory from its jurisdiction in order for it to join with its Canadian counterpart, to become independent and sovereign. A joint resolution in Congress, passed by a simple majority vote

---

iii   Rights to self-determination.

iv   And, if necessary, pass a statewide referendum, should a petition to overturn such a bill by popular vote acquire enough signatures in said state.

through regular order of business, is sufficient enough to achieve this. As the states will have already consented to border changes and the release of territory, all Congress would need to do is pass a joint resolution that would consent to the agreements made by the states, allow the executive branch to negotiate the transfer of federal property and sort out any other pertinent affairs, and allow the president to make an executive order designating the exact date and time the federal territory in question would officially be released, with the understanding that it would become part of the new country of Cascadia.

The process to achieve secession via consented release would be slightly different in Canada. First of all, the Supreme Court of Canada has ruled that there is constitutional precedence for secession. After Quebec attempted and failed to pass a referendum on secession in 1995, a case was brought before the Supreme Court questioning Quebec's right to achieve sovereignty through the referendum process. The Court reached a decision in 1998 and wrote the following:

> Our democratic institutions necessarily accommodate a continuous process of discussion and evolution, which is reflected in the constitutional right of each participant in the federation to initiate constitutional change. This right implies a reciprocal duty on the other participants to engage in discussions to address any legitimate initiative to change the constitutional order. *A clear majority vote in Quebec on a clear question in favour of seces-*

sion would confer democratic legitimacy on the se-cession initiative which all of the other participants in Confederation would have to recognize.

*Quebec could not, despite a clear referendum result, purport to invoke a right of self-determination to dictate the terms of a proposed secession to the other parties to the federation. The democratic vote, by however strong a majority, would have no legal effect on its own and could not push aside the prin-ciples of federalism and the rule of law, the rights of individuals and minorities, or the operation of democracy in the other provinces or in Canada as a whole._*Democratic rights under the Constitution cannot be divorced from constitutional obliga-tions. Nor, however, can the reverse proposition be accepted: the continued existence and operation of the Canadian constitutional order could not be indifferent to a clear expression of a clear majority of Quebecers that they no longer wish to remain in Canada. *The other provinces and the federal govern-ment would have no basis to deny the right of the government of Quebec to pursue secession should a clear majority of the people of Quebec choose that goal, so long as in doing so, Quebec respects the rights of others._*The negotiations that followed such a vote would address the potential act of se-cession as well as its possible terms should in fact secession proceed. There would be no conclusions predetermined by law on any issue. Negotiations would need to address the interests of the other provinces, the federal government and Quebec and indeed the rights of all Canadians both within and outside Quebec, and specifically the rights of minorities.

The negotiation process would require the reconciliation of various rights and obligations by negotiation between two legitimate majorities, namely, the majority of the population of Quebec, and that of Canada as a whole. A political majority at either level that does not act in accordance with the underlying constitutional principles puts at risk the legitimacy of its exercise of its rights, and the ultimate acceptance of the result by the international community.[80] (emphasis mine)

While a vote of the people in a province would solidify the legitimacy of secession, the process of actually seceding would not occur solely upon the result of such a vote. The order of secession would need to pass through Parliament in Ottawa, setting the conditions for negotiations regarding manners of logistics and consenting to the release of the area designated by the people.[v] In order for this to happen in the context of Cascadia, the provincial legislature of British Columbia would need to

---

v   The Clarity Act, passed after the Supreme Court ruling, also calls for a constitutional amendment to be passed in order for secession to occur legally. This would need to pass via Section 38 of the Constitution Act of 1982. This calls for an amendment's adoption by the House of Commons, the Senate, and two-thirds of the provincial legislative assemblies, representing at least 50% of the Canadian population.

pass a bill defining which parts of the province would secede to join its American counterparts and become part
of Cascadia, and which parts would remain in Canada,
either as a separate territory, a new province, or part of
the neighboring province of Alberta. Any part of British
Columbia east of the Canadian Rocky Mountains would
likely join the province of Alberta, since the total population of northeast British Columbia is likely considered
too small and insufficient to exist as its own province.[vi]
Once this bill passes through the provincial legislature
of British Columbia, a legally binding referendum would
be voted on by the people of British Columbia. Assuming
the support for Cascadia is already at an overwhelmingly
high margin, the legally binding referendum should pass
by a similar, indisputable margin of victory. Members of
Canadian Parliament, then, would need to consider the
following two questions after a successful referendum:
Was the question of secession clear? And was the margin
of support sufficient? If the answers to these two questions are in the affirmative, Parliament would then be
compelled to act and vote in favor of granting release
to the designated areas determined by the Cascadian
people. According to constitutional precedence, Parliament would have no grounds to vote against the result

---

vi   According to Section 43 of the Constitution Act of 1982, the
legislative body of Alberta would need to pass a bill accepting
the northeast portion of British Columbia to become part of Alberta (after a successful referendum by British Columbia), and
that agreement would need to pass through Canadian Parliament in Ottawa.

of the referendum. The order of secession passed by Parliament would outline the affairs that would need to be settled before secession could become official, designate the parties responsible for resolving these affairs, and give the power of setting the date for release of Cascadian territory from Canada to the prime minister or the governor general. Parliament would also need to pass a resolution, in accordance with Section 44 of the Constitution Act of 1982, to allow the small portion of the Yukon Territory's southern area that lies within the Cascadian region to also be released and become Cascadian territory. The map on the following page depicts these changes to political boundaries.[vii]

In addition to these processes in both countries, existing treaties between the United States and/or Canada with Native American or First Nation tribes will need to addressed and resolved on a case-by-case basis. Since Native American and First Nation tribes have some degree of sovereignty under federal and international law, that sovereignty must be respected during any legally binding process of securing independence for Cascadia. It is my sincere hope that most if not all of the Native American and First Nation organizations within the Cascadian region will help lead the way to securing a new independent Cas-

---

vii   This map shows Cascadian territory in relation to the present-day borders. The area in green is Cascadia. The areas in blue and red are parts of a state or province that would stay in its respective country but become part of another state or province because its former assembly would dissolve. The areas in gray would remain unchanged. This map is part of the Creative Commons, and no credit has been attributed to the creator.

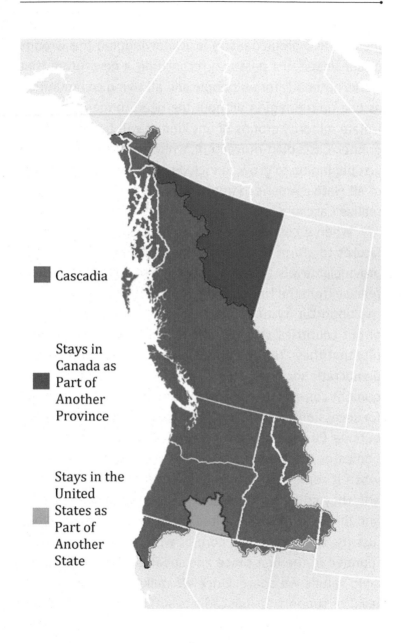

Cascadia

Stays in
Canada as
Part of
Another
Province

Stays in the
United
States as
Part of
Another
State

cadian nation. One inherent part of the Cascadian movement (and bioregionalism) is acknowledging the wrongs of our imperialist past and reconciling a new future that works optimally for all people and all living communities, as one united region without the need to marginalize or isolate minority groups of any kind. It will be vital for the greater Cascadian movement, while it is still young and just beginning to grow, to include and empower members of all Native American and First Nation tribes in order to realize Cascadia as truly one united region.

When it comes time for our respective federal legislatures to affirm the agreements made on our state and provincial levels, thereby consenting to Cascadia's orderly release from the United States and Canada, they will have the opportunity to prove to us as Cascadians, the rest of our countries' citizens, and the international community that they are the quintessential models for free and democratic societies. This is where the final part of my argument comes into play. We will need a moral argument for secession's justification that wins support from those outside Cascadia. And as flawed as the representative bodies of the United States and Canada are, especially when it comes to representing our interests as Cascadians, they still answer to the people. Our arguments for and justifications of a united, free Cascadia goes beyond just us. They go to the core of why our countries were founded in the first place and speak to the fundamental civic values we share. Once we make our case and the level of support for Cascadia is sufficient for us to complete the constitutional requirements I've outlined in this chapter, that same support will exist throughout much of the United States and Canada, outside the Cascadian region as well. Furthermore, even if the level of support among representatives in Congress and Parliament is lower than we desire, no legitimate and moral justification of any kind will exist for representatives to use against us. There indeed will be legitimate concerns, such as economic factors and concerns over international relations and the like, but these concerns should not, under any circumstance, deny or prevent Cascadians the moral right to self-determination; they are ephemeral and not fundamental to the notion of freedom.

Canada has the constitutional precedent set where, at the point when Parliament takes up the question of consent, members of Parliament legally couldn't deny the rights of Cascadians within its jurisdiction to pursue secession. Should Parliament vote against us, given these circumstances, the governor general of Canada would then have the authority to dissolve Parliament and call for new elections.

The United States does not have this same legal precedent that would, for all intents and purposes, force a vote of affirmation by Congress towards consented release. But given the level of popular support Cascadia would have given these circumstances, I firmly believe such a resolution would pass swiftly. The resolution need not be that long or complex, given that each state affected by this change would have already agreed on these new terms to which Congress would be consenting. I understand this entire process will be an unprecedented feat of coordination and logistics, but I have no doubt this process will be practical, legitimate, and pragmatic, once the irrefutable support for Cascadia exists.

To deny a united people the right to self-determination, after having used the constitutional democratic processes to achieve this possibility, would result in Congress and/or Parliament becoming nothing less than illegitimate foreign overlords interested only in maintaining the territory that representatives believe belongs to the institutions in Washington, DC, and/or Ottawa and not to the people. To do this would be to equate freedom with imperialist territorial claims irrespective of geography, no better than if Great Britain were to make the argument today that it would be more free if it had its former colonies back.

Our countries would prove themselves to be empires in which the freedoms of its citizens are subject to the whims of its elected officials. This would be contrary to the creed of every true American and Canadian. Any attempt to justify such an act of imperialism in this age of enlightened thought would fail miserably, as this sentiment would be shared by those throughout our two countries. If anything, any trust left in our federal institutions would permanently dissipate, and they would no longer maintain any moral authority whatsoever to govern legitimately.

Furthermore, the United States and Canada would receive enormous pressure from many of its allies to act in accordance with the democratic principles and the rule of law. How many allies and members of the global community in general would condemn or even sanction the United States and/or Canada if they were to deny our rights to self-determination as Cascadians, given these circumstances? I am confident in saying the answer would be much more than zero. Not only would we have moral justification on our side, we would have international law on our side as well. Resolution 1514 of the United Nation General Assembly states the following:

> All peoples have the right to self-determination; by virtue of that right they freely determine their political status and freely pursue their economic, social and cultural development ...

> Immediate steps shall be taken, in Trust and Non-Self-Governing Territories or all other territories which have not yet attained independence, to transfer all powers to the peoples of those territories, without any conditions or reservations, in accordance with their freely expressed will and desire, without any distinction as to race, creed or colour, in order to enable them to enjoy complete independence and freedom ...

> All States shall observe faithfully and strictly the provisions of the Charter of the United Nations, the Universal Declaration of Human Rights and the present Declaration on the basis of equality, non-interference in the internal affairs of all States, and respect for the sovereign rights of all peoples and their territorial integrity.[81]

Far too many American and Canadian citizens, in and outside of Cascadia, will support the fundamental argu-

ments for freedom and self-determination. Even if powerful interests in Washington, DC, or Ottawa do not wish
to consent to Cascadia's release, our federal institutions
will have far too much lose, given these circumstances, by
trying to thwart our efforts. Our federal institutions will
uphold the values they were founded upon and grant the
right of Cascadians to realize our own self-determination.
Just as Cascadia was once free and whole, cared for and
protected by its inhabitants who were truly elemental to
its environment, so will it be again in the context of a
brand new veracity in the twenty-first century.[viii]

Right now, this whole process seems highly unlikely.

---

viii   There will be a time of transition after both federal governments approve the bills consenting to the secession of territory. A unified transitional authority of some sort representing
Cascadia would need to work with both the governments of the
United States and Canada to resolve all other logistical matters
before Cascadia can become an independent country. These
matters would include, among other things, the transfer of
Canadian or American federal land or property to be inherited
by Cascadians, the transfer of money or debt according to the
proper financial burden of the Cascadian territory, creating and
coordinating new border patrols and border-crossing areas, the
designation and allocation of any shared natural resources, and
treaties of alliance and friendship. During this time of transition,
Cascadian territory would be effectively run by the authorities
or bodies of power determined by the Cascadian people, even
though the president of the United States and the prime minister
of Canada would still be the heads of government that have ultimate jurisdiction over Cascadian territory. Once enough matters
of transition have been resolved and agreed upon by Cascadian,
Canadian, and American parties, a date for independence would
be set to transfer full rights of sovereignty to a new Cascadian
country.

Even if you see that it meets the requirements of both the United States and Canadian Constitutions, you may be skeptical. I would agree that right now, it does seem unlikely. A movement unified across an international border to achieve secession from two countries has never been done in this manner. But the improbability of completing this process of secession, as we analyze it in the present day, does not change the fact that we're Cascadian or that this course of action may be right. Our movement is just beginning. Most Cascadians don't even know they're Cascadian yet. If bioregionalism is correct—and our bioregional ethos is indeed good and true and able to unite the people of this region, regardless of differences in historical background, culture, geography, spirituality, or ideology—then our movement will thrive in due course. The Cascadian identity will grow, and the support for a new, independent Cascadia will grow with it. If we work hard and efficiently, we will unite across state, provincial, and international borders to further our cause outside of politics, solidifying what it truly means to be Cascadian and live by Cascadian values. We can grow our movement efficiently in this age of instant information, sharing ideas and solutions to our problems. Discussion about the possibility for Cascadian independence will occur among Americans and Canadians within Cascadia, as well as outside of it. New possibilities never considered before will be thoroughly debated and analyzed by many across this continent. We can take our movement as it exists right now and foster its spread throughout the entire region in a single generation, over the course of the next one or two decades. Then, before we know it, the prospect for independence—for completing this process of legal steps, which at the present time seems improbable—will become very possible and, perhaps, even inevitable. In time, the idea of secession will not be a taboo subject where we, as Cascadians, are the hostile reactionaries or naïve ideologues trying to fight with Canada and the United States.

Cascadia was once the child, now grown up in the context of our two countries, which has learned to see and experience the world in a different way from our parents. We'll have fully come into our own and will be ready to move out of our parents' houses, so to speak. We may be fundamentally different and seek to be independent, as is natural and right, but that doesn't mean we'll stop being part of the family.

Taking this movement from its early beginnings in our present day to its finality and achieving a new country will require hard work, focus, dedication, wisdom, unity, and persistence. We will make mistakes and stumble along in our journey. We will also keep an open mind and learn from our mistakes, ensuring the movement does not falter. We will encounter adversity and obstacles. If our movement is good and true and our dedication and work are sufficient, then we will overcome any such adversity and obstacles that come our way. We must never give in to fear or feel we need to resort to exclusionary or violent ideology in order to achieve progress. We must be ever mindful and accept what we cannot change, have the courage and solidarity to change what we can, and have the wisdom to know the difference between the two. We will grow, we will learn, and we will, in time, achieve our goal, making our vision for a new Cascadia a reality. Cascadia is calling to us. We are listening. Now we must act and work together.

7. FORWARD

Something is happening in Cascadia. For the past four decades, the idea of Cascadia has been a dream during the quiet stillness of night, fleeting and jumbled in our minds as we sleep. But like an epiphany realized after a dream so powerful and vivid, we have woken up with clarity and a drive that will change the course of history. Dawn has broken; it is time for us to take this clarity, take this drive, and to turn dreams into reality. Beyond the noise of political bickering, beyond the pomp and circumstance in Washington, DC, and Ottawa, a genuine movement has already begun in the northwest corner of this great continent. Citizens young and old are exploring what it means to truly thrive, according to the place where they live. More individuals are turning to answers outside their country's capitals to solve the issues that face them, finding ways to embrace a new vision for a positive future. Living sustainably, conserving resources and energy, embracing local communities and culture, shedding the bonds of postcolonial conformity, thinking in new and different ways, sharing innovative ideas yet untested, living open and honestly, respecting diversity, maximizing individual potential, asking "why not?" to bold ideas—each of these conceptions is experienced in our daily lives as part of being Cascadian. We express them according to our own intuition, but we experience them as one unified region, in distinct ways that set us apart from every other region on this continent. "Cascadia," as an idea, has already become popular in social realms,[i] which in turn have become parts of the Cascadian identity we witness today. They speak to our unique expressions of community and values. These social expressions are just the beginning of a movement both monumental and defining.

In this book, I have provided an argument that attempts to justify the natural inherency of Cascadia. A summary of my argument can be broken down into five distinct parts:

1. Cascadia is a unique and fundamentally different region on this continent that provides for the characteristics and guiding principles of society—an ethos—that are equally as unique and fundamentally different.

2. This uniqueness is directly influenced from the natural elements of the region we live in; it is as permanent as our bioregional environment.

3. The notion of freedom we need, as individuals and a society simultaneously, is a balance of liberties determined in part by the bioregionally inherent ethos we experience.

---

i   For example, soccer, music, festivals, conventions, journalism, social networking, gaming, etc.

4. We are a divergent region that cannot attain the notions of freedom we need in our current federal structures. They are incapable of adequately representing our interests as Cascadians, and it is thus inevitable that we will succumb to the demands of the more powerful, influential regions in our two countries.

5. There is a practical, pragmatic, nonviolent, and legal path forward to be released from our current federal institutions and to secure our right to self-determination.

It is my sincere hope that all who read this book will consider a new rationality and a new perspective that I have put forth, whether a long-time supporter of Cascadia, an ardent skeptic, or an indifferent citizen just looking for answers. Once you do, I urge you to explore these justifications and possibilities further to come to your own conclusions and not limit yourself to believing just in finite possibilities. After all, it was not too long before starting my research for this book that I adamantly denied bioregionalism as anything but a fad of environmentalists and vehemently opposed any idea that even hinted at secession.

After spending the past few years exploring my own biases and rationalities that I had always assumed to be true, I have come to conclusions about who we are as a society, what's truly ailing our status quo, and how we can create a new status quo that is more beneficial and sustainable. I'm not insinuating that all who read this book should agree with everything I say. I'm simply suggesting that if I can go from frustrated doubter to confident believer, then anyone can. I am now part of the Cascadia movement, and I look forward to playing my part in fostering it and helping transform the assumptions of Cascadian society and its possibilities. Ultimately, I hope the citizens of this region feel empowered to act for sensible yet fundamental change. The Cascadian movement is not a reactionary one perpetrated by fools who don't like the results of an election. This is a proactive movement of affirmation to do what's best for our region, united across political ideologies, religious beliefs, socioeconomic backgrounds, and international borders. We are not a country yet, but we are a nation of people, united through our bioregion, working to change our status quo.

Our movement is at the stage of spreading awareness of what Cascadia is, as it exists now—what sets us apart from everyone else in the United States and Canada and what it means to identify as Cascadian. It is true that we feel frustration with our current federal systems of governance, along with the lack of representation of our values in the common narratives about what it means to be American or Canadian. But our desire to strive for something new is not done out of an exclusionary philosophy towards others; it stems from the fact that our countries' statuses quo are holding us back and not allowing us to fulfill our potential as we were meant to be, as one united region. I'm sure many of us can attest that we do not dislike the idea of America or Canada. We still honor and respect the national identities we currently hold, but we know the idea of Cascadia is right for us. We are simultaneously pro-America and pro-Canada while supporting this vision for Cascadia.

The opportunities we have as Cascadians in areas of economy, culture, ecology, science, and more are abundant, waiting for us to take advantage of them. Furthermore, we can see the draining of resources and finances that currently serve the impatient and unsteady interests of regions to our east. How long do we sit idle, content to remain in federal systems we know are not sustainable? How long do we wait before the rest of the continent runs out of their resources, moves past the point of no return, and looks to Cascadia to sustain an incompatible lifestyle of individual gratification and overconsumption? We must do our part to protect our interests, replenish our resources, and lead by example. We must unite as an ecologically bound region to enact our values of conservation and sustainability to help temper the potentially disastrous effects of global warming. We don't have all the answers to the problems we face, but we do have new ideas, based on our ways of life and our rationality influenced from the region in which we live. We've already started this process and are making progress. Cascadia is best suited to accomplish a task never done before. We will rise and meet the challenge.

Doing this will require evolving our understanding of the term "nationalism." Again, I state that Cascadia is equal to a nation in which its people conform to a unifying ethos and hold the same guiding principles true to heart, regardless of the color of their skin, the religion they subscribe to, or where they were born. For too long, human beings have understood nationalism to be an exclusive, divisive notion that does more to separate people than unite them. If Cascadians are to truly come together as one, we must change our idea of nationhood, or national identity, to one of empowerment and inclusion. This inclusive model has been dubbed "civic nationalism," in which the national community purposefully does not impose restriction on any human-identifier criteria.[82] Civic nationalism affords anyone the choice to join a national community and embody that society's ethos.[83] The result is a society made of persons unified in common commitment towards each other and their shared ideals.[84] I believe the concept of "civic nationalism" fits perfectly with bioregionalism; anyone who chooses to call Cascadia home and become an inhabitant of this region—staying true to the "terrain of consciousness," as Peter Berg would have said, and choosing to be part of a shared ecologically based political body—should be considered as subscribing to Cascadian nationhood and, thereby, being part of a united Cascadian nation. The one civic belief that I hold above all others and one that I hope spreads throughout Cascadia is that "nationalism" should not be defined by ethnicity, race, language, religion, political ideology, or any other auxiliary characteristic. The nationhood that defines a society and to which its individuals subscribe should be determined by its common geography and common ethos, naturally delineated by the environment in which it resides, regardless of those auxiliary characteristics by which human beings tend to label and differentiate each other.

In other words, we need to evolve our understanding of nationalism to be an idea based in the concept of place, not people. This belief is at the heart of bioregionalism. If a nation relies on the exclusivity of race or ethnicity or on the hegemony of religion or ideology, it does not deserve to exist, nor can it exist peacefully. These characteristics bring diversity and new ideas to society. They give nationhood strength and opportunity for growth. They can be things that individuals take pride in, but they should not prevent the chance for someone to become part of a national society.

For Cascadia, this means that one's ethnicity, language, political ideology, or religion should not automatically exclude her or him from conforming to Cascadia's bioregional ethos. Our goal should not be to turn back the clock on social progress and return Cascadia to the social order that existed prior to American and Canadian settlement. Our goal should be to take Cascadian society as it exists now, work to break down social barriers of exclusion and prejudice, and allow a true fusion of our diverse array of cultural characteristics to form a unifying way of life that is truly and uniquely "Cascadian." This does not mean we should allow dominant cultural trends to wipe out all others, forcing them to conform. This also does not mean we should strive for diversity that exists only if our differences are segregated into areas in which minority trends are hegemonic in certain places and nowhere to be found in others. We need actual diversity, in which our cities, towns, and neighborhoods are truly reflective of who we are as a regional society. For example, the fewer differences there are in shared ways of life between the bustling urban metropolis and the rural aboriginal community, the better off we'll be. From the entrepreneur to the community organizer, from the logger to the environmental activist, from the First Nation member to those with no aboriginal background at all, from the lifelong resident to the immigrant—we can all be Cascadian in this place. We all have the potential within us to make Cascadia our own and become true inhabitants of this region. Each of us has something positive to offer this region and our movement to realize our own self-determination.

This vision is made possible through bioregionalism. The phenomenon of naturally-influenced ethos and regional differentiation is a fact we should embrace. Ignoring this reality is futile, and attempting to overcome this reality is as self-destructive as attempting to destroy the awesome power of nature that forged it. While we shouldn't separate ourselves based on differences in ethnic background or skin color, we should be able to unite as a national community and truly be ourselves. Right now, we can't be a collective self, as we were truly meant to be, because our federal institutions of power and international borders prevent us from doing so. We must work to change this reality. The maps of the United States and Canada were drawn generations ago by politicians and diplomats concerned with the influence of their respective empires. The geographic overexpansion resulted in convoluted messes of regional ethos (plural) fighting against one another. These convoluted messes are our current "national" identities. The map of Cascadia, however, was drawn by a force much more powerful than any group of human beings. Its identity is rooted in an environment of mountains, evergreen forests, and rain. It's waiting for the day it can truly be itself—when we can truly be ourselves, no longer torn in two. In this sense, healthy boundaries that allow Cascadia to unite and separate itself as an independent entity will be necessary for the peaceful coexistence of national societies to thrive. The opportunity we have today is to recognize these issues are present because of bioregionalism and resolve them on the fundamental level through forming a new political reality.

It's not that individuals on this continent do not wish to be united under a single national entity; it's that we weren't meant to be. Speaking personally for a moment as a religious man—and I'm sure my sentiment can be amended to fit your spirituality or worldview—if God wanted us to be politically one and the same, surely s/he would have forged this planet with a uniform environment, so even if we as people are diverse, we would experience the effects of human action and interaction in the same surroundings, perpetuating a uniform system of values and culture. Obviously, that's not the planet we live on. Nature has created a planet with diverse, unique, distinct regions with different environments, different living systems, and different surroundings, each of which creates different ways of experiencing life. What is true and right for a society living in one region may not be true and right for a society living in another, at least in terms of politics and governance. This does not mean Cascadians should aim to isolate and shelter themselves from the rest of the world; it simply means we should be able to be true to ourselves and our environment, and guide our regionally based society on our own terms without being subservient to the exploitive, alien influences of other regions.

The *ultimate* goal of our broad movement is not secession; that's simply a mechanism to achieve our ultimate goal of creating the Cascadian reality we wish to enable. I do believe, however, that political separation from our two present countries is both inevitable and pragmatic. It will not be accomplished out of some grand, romanticized struggle for freedom. Rather, it will be a practical solution to the fundamental issues that face us as a region and as a continent. Like businesses that have overgrown to dominate a market and diminish competition, the United States and Canada have over-expanded to become monopolies on this continent, specifically disrupting the unity and potential of the Cascadian region. And just like monopolies that break down into smaller entities that compete with each other and create opportunity and value for a much broader scale of people, the United States and Canada can give way to new opportunity and value that only a united Cascadia can provide. Once Americans and Canadians alike realize this practicality, and the broader Cascadian movement has grown to the point where it truly embodies our ethos throughout the entire region, the only remaining obstacle to achieving political autonomy will be the logistics presented by our democratic processes. But until that point comes, no regional autonomy or unity will occur until an overwhelming, irrefutable majority of Cascadians say they want it to occur.

Secession will require the consent of not just our states, provinces, and territories but our federal systems as well. And according to the doctrine of federalism, that's exactly how it should be. We are not "slaves" who need to revolt and dominate "the master." We are not utterly without freedom in our status quo. Freedom is not a status that either exists or doesn't; it's a balance of liberties that create a status of freedom that can exist in varying degrees. Fundamental change, especially on this type of monumental scale, was not meant to happen with a simple majority of only those directly affected in the geographic area in question. Rather, it was meant to happen with the consent of those within a federal system, so that legitimacy can be recognized and established without the need for violent conflict. We have constitutional mechanisms in both the United States and Canada that allow us the opportunity to secede amicably and peacefully from our respective unions. These mechanisms, while not explicitly written out in the form of a how-to manual, were created so that violent revolution would never again be necessary to secure freedom and self-determination on this continent.

We will be the first region to complete this process successfully, not to mention that we'll do it in two different countries. It will not be easy to get to the point where enough public support exists to move forward with the legal processes of secession, nor will the logistical processes of achieving it once the support exists be easy to accomplish. But we will accomplish these tasks to create the Cascadia we dream of, inspiring ourselves and the world with new possibilities.

I want to emphasize that the arguments I make in this book, particularly regarding the pursuit of political independence, are ones I make for Cascadia only. As I subscribe to the regional nationhood of Cascadia, I believe I have the right to argue for Cascadia. And as I do not subscribe to any other regional nationhood, it would be inappropriate and naïve of me to attempt to make any similar arguments for any other region(s) on this continent. It may be that bioregionalism is realized by more than just Cascadians, and other regional nations on this continent pursue a new political reality as well. If that is to be, then it must be argued for and pursued by those who subscribe to the identity of their respective regional nations. However, in the scenario of Cascadia's achieving independence, this does not mean other regional nations will automatically follow suit. As I proposed earlier, I see the Cascadian ethos as the primary divergent ethos that contributes to the conglomerations of the American and Canadian identities. It is entirely possible that the shared commonalities between the other regional ethos (plural) in each of our countries will become more apparent and more cohesive once Cascadia is removed from the equation. In this scenario, other regions, should they subscribe more so to being American or Canadian than their re-spective regional identity, would not necessarily pursue independence themselves. This should be taken into consideration by any who believe the secession of Cas-cadia would lead to the "downfall" of the United States or Canada. With the understanding of how our countries' identities are composed, there's no basis for any such fear becoming reality, simply because Cascadia secedes.

If, however, the future does give way to bioregional-ism and regional countries, thereby ending the existence of the United States and Canada, that does not mean these countries will have failed. If these countries allow for the peaceful evolution of our great experiments in freedom and democracy, then I argue these experiments that are the United States and Canada will have concluded as the most profound and successful examples in human his-tory. If anything, the United States and Canada will only "fail" and collapse should the federal powers attempt to thwart the democratic liberties of their regional nations and forcibly coerce them into remaining part of a union of which they no longer wish to be a part.[ii] Any regional evolution in our existing federal paradigm should not be feared or seen as a threat to freedom or democracy. If we are to truly reject imperialism and exploitation, such evolution should be welcomed and explored.

When the time comes to seriously consider pro-ceeding with secession, there will likely be some key

---

ii   Assuming, of course, each region pursues such indepen-dence according to their country's (or countries') constitutional principles.

sticking points preventing certain people from supporting Cascadia. Some might question this ideal of a
bioregional country and whether or not it should be the
next step we take as a united region. Some might not
feel adapting this new idea and making it our own is
worth the risk of starting a new experiment in realizing
self-determination. They'd rather stick with the systems
we have now out of fear of the unknown. I have but one
response to this notion: I pray that fear will not be the
reason that stops us from coming together and moving
forward with practical and pragmatic solutions, even if
they are untested. The only thing that overcomes fear is
knowledge and understanding. It will be the job of those
who find reason in the arguments for Cascadia to share
their thoughts and experiences with others in this region.

Others might feel that there are just too many obstacles with regard to secession, such as economic, legal,
and resource-based ramifications. To this I say that international borders will change, allowing us as Cascadians
to fulfill our sense of self-determination, but the culture
and commerce of this region will not simply disappear
from the rest of the continent. Logistical obstacles that
come with international relations and trade should not
be a blockade to pursuing independence.

Others, particularly in the United States, may feel
that attempting to secede will result in war, just as it
did in 1861. I emphasize the point that it is proper and
appropriate to work the existing federal systems and
constitutional principles in order to achieve secession.
This is something the old Confederacy never attempted

to do before responding to federal pressure with violent force.[iii] Pursuing consented release from the United States should not be feared in this manner—to use the words of Thomas Paine, "for there are ten times more to dread from a patched up [connection] than from independence."[85] Still others may feel, as I did shortly before beginning my research for this book, that seceding from the United States and Canada to make Cascadia a reality would be a treasonous betrayal to the idea of freedom, no better than the old Confederacy that attempted to secede from the United States and sparked the Civil War. To this I say that freedom is not inherent to any country or constitutional document. These things are supposed to exist in order to enhance and protect the freedom that belongs to the people. Once a country stops being able to do this adequately for some of its people, it is the duty of those within that country to make the necessary changes so that freedom for its entire people can thrive peacefully. Secession will merely result in a change of social contracts; it does not sever Cascadia from the spirit or the shared ideals that have made the United States and Canada great. We believe in the civil creeds of freedom, justice, and self-determination that caused colonists to rebel against oppression and pioneers to search for new possibilities. We have learned from our successes and

---

iii   The Confederacy was also guilty of what is now universally considered the moral abomination of institutionalized slavery. This is an entirely different argument but one that further proves the point that Cascadia is not and would not be the same as the Confederacy.

our failures as young countries establishing themselves in times of uncertainty and adversity. We have shared in the prosperity, hardship, joy, and grief with our fellow citizens through the best of times and the worst of times. Nothing—and I mean nothing—can take away our shared humanity and our shared history.

Before bringing this book to a close, I wish to share with you my vision and hopes for the Cascadian movement, of which I consider myself a part. Our movement must be broad, across many areas of our daily lives, as well as sweeping across the entirety of our geography. Ultimately, as I've mentioned, Cascadia isn't about politics or secession; it's about instilling a way of life that is true and sustainable to this region. Politics and its consequences are simply by-products of that goal. The importance and strength to our movement comes from all the things we experience in Cascadia that make life worth living, not politics. Therefore, we must never strive for the rigidness and impossibility of "ideological purity," nor should we ever feel the need to exclude fellow Cascadians, who desire the same future for our region, from the movement because their political views differ from others who are involved. It is human nature to exclude others we disagree with because of the discomfort caused from having to reconsider or amend one's worldview. We must resist this primitive aspect of our human nature and actively work to understand the rationales of our fellow Cascadians with whom we may not necessarily see eye-to-eye. We must resist the temptation to see contradictory opinions as threats. We will have differences of opinion and different ideas on how to achieve the future we desire. But in this unified region, our political differences can and will be reconciled. Compromise—the true hope of any democratic society—will be absolutely necessary to achieve what we desire. And by "compromise," I do not mean the foolish process we see so often of routinely watering down or weakening collective agreements to appease zealous opponents or to not disrupt the status quo too much so that one's supporters don't get too upset. True compromise—the joining of bold and brave ideas through discourse and debate and the subsequent agreement to utilize the best parts of these ideas in the face of uncertainty or adversity—is the most courageous and heroic feat any society can achieve. We must work together, realizing that no single person will ever be 100% right, that our choices are not "either/or," and that the tangible specifics of Cascadia's system of governance and representation will work themselves out when the appropriate time arrives.

We will not get to where we want to be with a single ideology. We will not eliminate all of our prejudices and dissipate all of our fears through coercion or "purity." We must *never* mistake absolutism of conviction for principle; to do so would be to unintentionally assert an infallibility of certain human conditions or political ideologies. Should we choose to embrace the reality of our bioregional unity and our common ethos, focusing on the diverse qualities that make this region so special, the politics of Cascadia will naturally be worked through as a subsequent effect of our work in the broader Cascadian movement. When the time comes for political independence, we will provide a more applicable system that works across our region, utilizing the strength of our common ethos and our local diversities that make us unique.

For those of you who see what I see and feel what I feel, whether a longtime supporter or a newly inspired Cascadian, in full agreement with my arguments or not, I implore you to be the future you wish to see in this world. Talk to people about our region, what it means to be Cascadian, and how we don't have to accept a dire fate of political gridlock, financial collapse, or global deterioration. We can change our region's status quo for the better. If you truly believe that and are willing to work for it, that's exactly what we'll do. Many disheartened and disenchanted citizens of this region feel stuck, as if their future is gray, at best, and don't know what to do about it. Many in this region look up to the stars and stripes of the American flag or the red maple leaf of the Canadian flag and feel a noticeable void. You, like me, may be one of those people. One day—hopefully, soon—that void will be filled in the form of our Douglas fir banner of green, white, and blue waving alongside those of our American and Canadian cousins.[iv]

This is our symbol of our future. It starts with one very simple first step of empowerment. Instead of saying "Pacific Northwest," say "Cascadia."

iv   Image credit: Patch Perryman © 2014. Used with permission from Patch Perryman.

The "Pacific Northwest" is a nameless object at the distant corner of Atlantic empires, an object of second thought to the power centers in Washington DC & Ottawa. We have a name: We are Cascadians! And we have a home: It is called Cascadia! By giving ourselves and our home a name, we begin the process of empowering ourselves and restoring the land as a place of home and sacredness, and not a place for 'resource extraction' for empire or greed.[86]

I believe with every fiber of my being that we will change the course of history for the better. If we don't believe we can do this, no one else will believe either, and no one will work for it. Cascadia has been a dream in the wee hours of the morning, appearing in the distance and calling our names while we sleep. But dawn has broken, and our day to achieve this new reality has begun. We are awake with full eyes, a clear mind, and a desire to do something true and great. Like the Americans of generations past who argued for their independence, we realize that this fundamental change that allows Cascadia to truly be free must be made. Once again, I give you the words of Thomas Paine in his argument titled *Common Sense*:

[Everything] that is right or natural pleads for separation. The blood of the slain, the weeping voice of nature cries, 'TIS TIME TO PART. Even the distance at which the Almighty hath placed England and America, is a strong and natural proof, that the authority of one, over the other, was never the design of heaven ...

These proceedings may at first appear strange and difficult; but, like all other steps which we have already passed over, will in a little time become familiar and agreeable; and, until an independence is declared, the Continent will feel itself like a man who continues putting off some unpleasant business from day to day, yet knows it must be done, hates to set about it, wishes it over, and is continually haunted with the thoughts of its necessity.[87]

The circumstances may differ slightly, but the rationale remains as true as ever. In fact, replace "England and America" with "Cascadia and Washington, DC/Ottawa," and then replace "until an independence is declared" with "until a consented release is achieved," and the argument is basically the same now as it was more than two hundred years ago. It is my hope that the arguments presented in my book will resonate with all those in Cascadia looking for "common sense."

From the coast of the Pacific Ocean to the Great Continental Divide;

From the Salish Sea and the Puget Sound to the Willamette Valley;

From Cape Mendocino and the state of Jefferson to Mt. Logan and the Alaskan Panhandle;

From the Snake River to the Columbia River to the Fraser River;

To every city, community, and individual in this region;

We are Cascadians. Say it; embrace it.

Like the mighty rivers that serve as the lifeblood of our region, we will be the force of nature that gives life to our vision as we embody our ethos and work towards a new future. And when we have done this, we'll look up in the twilight and see the Cascadian banner of blue, white, and green, waving in the wind over our land—united, independent, and free.

This is Cascadia.

END NOTE CONCERNING
THE CASCADIAN FLAG

The Cascadian flag was designed by Alexander Baretich during the academic year of 1994–1995 and represents the bioregion of Cascadia. The following was written by Mr. Baretich with respect to the use of his design in publications:

"This design should not to be used for hate (1) or exploitation (2).

1.) Hate speech being defined as words, depictions and actions generated against an individual or group based on ethnicity, religious affiliation (or non-religious association or identity), race, gender identity, sexuality (from orientation to mutually consenting adult activities), familial structure, mobility, educational background (or "lack" of institutional education), caste or economic situation (class) and so forth. Hate speech also may be disguised as "White Pride" or nationalism. The Cascadian flag by Alexander Baretich does not represent any of these forms of hate and should not be used to represent such hate.

2.) Exploitation being defined by the actions of treating someone unfairly in order to benefit from their work or the violating of Nature for profit at the expense of causing ecological harm. The use of the flag should not be contrary to the ideas of bioregionalism.

The symbolism of the Cascadian flag:

The blue represents the moisture rich sky above and Pacific Ocean along with the Salish Sea, lakes and other inland waters. Our home is of continuous cascading waters flowing from our sky and mountains back to the Pacific. For Cascadia is a land of falling water from the Pacific to the western slopes of the Rockies where water cycles as vapor and then rain and snow to run through creek and river back to the Pacific. The white is for the snow and clouds which are the catalyst of water changing from one state of matter to another. From liquid into vapor (mist and clouds) and from vapor into solid (ice and snow) and melting back to liquid or vapor. The green is the forests and fields which too carry life giving water through our biodiverse land. The lone standing Douglas fir symbolizes endurance, defiance and resilience against fire, flood, catastrophic change and even against anthropocentric man."

(ENDNOTES)

1   P. Berg, Reinhabiting a Separate Country: A Bioregional Anthology of Northern California, San Francisco: Planet Drum Foundation, 1978.

2   D. Alexander, "Bioregionalism: The Need for a Firmer Theoretical Foundation," *The Trumpeter Journal of Ecosophy,* vol. 13, no. 3, 1996.

3   J. Barman, "Cascadia Once Upon a Time," in *Cascadia: The Elusive Utopia - Exploring the Spirit of the Pacific Northwest,* Vancouver, Ronsdale Press, 2009, pp. 89-104.

4   C. Hare and K. T. Poole, "The Polarization of Contemporary American Politics," University of Georgia - School of Public and International Affairs: Department of Political Science, Athens, 2013.

5   S. Perlo-Freeman and C. Solmirano, "Trends in World Military Expenditure, 2013," SIPRI, Stockholm, 2014.

6   OECD, "PISA 2012 Results in Focus: What 15-year-olds know and what they can do with what they know," 2013.

7   M. Henry, D. A. Cortes, S. Morris and A. Associates, "The 2013 Annual Homeless Assessment Report (AHAR) to Congress - Part 1: Point-in-Time Estimates of Homelessness," US Department of Housing and Urban Development - Office of Community Planning and Development, Washington, 2013.

8   D. Wintonyk, "West is best? B.C. residents identify most with U.S. West Coasters," CTV Vancouver, Vancouver, 2014.

9   Canada - House of Commons, "Ed. Hansard, Number 087: Contents," in *39th Parliament - 1st Session,* Ottawa, 2006.

10 G. Hoekstra, "More Than Half of B.C. Residents Oppose Northern Gateway Pipeline, Poll Suggests," Vancouver Sun, Vancouver, 2012.

11 I. Das, "Poll Finds Most B.C. Residents Still Strongly Oppose Enbridge Oil Tanker and Pipeline Proposal," Desmog Canada, Victoria, 2014.

12 P. Moskowitz, "Tailings Ponds Are the Biggest Environmental Disaster You've Never Heard of," Vice News, Brooklyn, 2014.

13 M. Wexler, "Conjectures on Workplace Spirituality in Cascadia," in *Cascadia: The Elusive Utopia - Exploring the Spirit of the Pacific Northwest*, Vancouver, Ronsdale Press, 2009, pp. 215-239.

14 J. Barman, "Cascadia Once Upon a Time," in *Cascadia: The Elusive Utopia - Exploring the Spirit of the Pacific Northwest*, Vancouver, Ronsdale Press, 2009, pp. 89-104.

15 J. Barman, "Cascadia Once Upon a Time," in *Cascadia: The Elusive Utopia - Exploring the Spirit of the Pacific Northwest*, Vancouver, Ronsdale Press, 2009, pp. 89-104.

16 J. Barman, "Cascadia Once Upon a Time," in *Cascadia: The Elusive Utopia - Exploring the Spirit of the Pacific Northwest*, Vancouver, Ronsdale Press, 2009, pp. 89-104.

17 J. Barman, "Cascadia Once Upon a Time," in *Cascadia: The Elusive Utopia - Exploring the Spirit of the Pacific Northwest*, Vancouver, Ronsdale Press, 2009, pp. 89-104.

18 M. Wexler, "Conjectures on Workplace Spirituality in Cascadia," in *Cascadia: The Elusive Utopia - Exploring the Spirit of the Pacific Northwest*, Vancouver, Ronsdale Press, 2009, pp. 215-239.

19 M. Wexler, "Conjectures on Workplace Spirituality in Cascadia," in *Cascadia: The Elusive Utopia - Exploring the Spirit of the Pacific Northwest*, Vancouver, Ronsdale Press, 2009, pp. 215-239.

20 M. Wexler, "Conjectures on Workplace Spirituality in Cascadia," in *Cascadia: The Elusive Utopia - Exploring the Spirit of*

the Pacific Northwest, Vancouver, Ronsdale Press, 2009, pp. 215-239.

21 M. Wexler, "Conjectures on Workplace Spirituality in Cascadia," in *Cascadia: The Elusive Utopia - Exploring the Spirit of the Pacific Northwest,* Vancouver, Ronsdale Press, 2009, pp. 215-239.

22 M. Wexler, "Conjectures on Workplace Spirituality in Cascadia," in *Cascadia: The Elusive Utopia - Exploring the Spirit of the Pacific Northwest,* Vancouver, Ronsdale Press, 2009, pp. 215-239.

23 M. Wexler, "Conjectures on Workplace Spirituality in Cascadia," in *Cascadia: The Elusive Utopia - Exploring the Spirit of the Pacific Northwest,* Vancouver, Ronsdale Press, 2009, pp. 215-239.

24 M. Wexler, "Conjectures on Workplace Spirituality in Cascadia," in *Cascadia: The Elusive Utopia - Exploring the Spirit of the Pacific Northwest,* Vancouver, Ronsdale Press, 2009, pp. 215-239.

25 M. Wexler, "Conjectures on Workplace Spirituality in Cascadia," in *Cascadia: The Elusive Utopia - Exploring the Spirit of the Pacific Northwest,* Vancouver, Ronsdale Press, 2009, pp. 215-239.

26 Indiana University-Purdue University Indianapolis, *Religious Affiliation in the Pacific Northwest and the Nation,* Indianapolis: Polis Center - North American Religion Atlas, 2004.

27 P. O'Connell Killen, "Patterns of the Past, Prospects for the Future: Religion in the None Zone," in *Religion & Public Life in the Pacific Northwest: The None Zone,* Walnut Creek, AltaMira Press, 2004, pp. 9-20.

28 M. Kaemingk, "Cascadian Culture: Grasping a Slippery Salmon," Christ & Cascadia, Seattle, 2013.

29 M. Wexler, "Conjectures on Workplace Spirituality in Cascadia," in *Cascadia: The Elusive Utopia - Exploring the Spirit of the Pacific Northwest,* Vancouver, Ronsdale Press, 2009, pp. 215-239.

30 M. Wexler, "Conjectures on Workplace Spirituality in Cascadia," in *Cascadia: The Elusive Utopia - Exploring the Spirit of the Pacific Northwest*, Vancouver, Ronsdale Press, 2009, pp. 215-239.

31 M. Wexler, "Conjectures on Workplace Spirituality in Cascadia," in *Cascadia: The Elusive Utopia - Exploring the Spirit of the Pacific Northwest*, Vancouver, Ronsdale Press, 2009, pp. 215-239.

32 T. Jefferson, *Letter to John Jacob Astor, Esq.*, Monticello, 1813.

33 J. Barman, "Cascadia Once Upon a Time," in *Cascadia: The Elusive Utopia - Exploring the Spirit of the Pacific Northwest*, Vancouver, Ronsdale Press, 2009, pp. 89-104.

34 J. Barman, "Cascadia Once Upon a Time," in *Cascadia: The Elusive Utopia - Exploring the Spirit of the Pacific Northwest*, Vancouver, Ronsdale Press, 2009, pp. 89-104.

35 J. Barman, "Cascadia Once Upon a Time," in *Cascadia: The Elusive Utopia - Exploring the Spirit of the Pacific Northwest*, Vancouver, Ronsdale Press, 2009, pp. 89-104.

36 City-Data.com, "Multnomah County, Oregon (OR) Religion Statistics Profile - Portland, Gresham, Troutdale, Fairview, Wood Village," 2011.

37 City-Data.com, "Denver County, Colorado (CO) Religion Statistics Profile - Denver," 2011.

38 P. O'Connell Killen, "Memory, Novelty and Possibility in This Place," in *Cascadia: The Elusive Utopia - Exploring the Spirit of the Pacific Northwest*, Vancouver, Ronsdale Press, 2009, pp. 65-85.

39 W. R. Fisher, Human Communication as Narration: Toward a Philosophy of Reason, Value, and Action, Columbia: University of South Carolina Press, 1989.

40 C. B. Corcoran, D. Hess and M. Sweet, Directors, *Occupied Cascadia*. [Film]. Cascadia: Cascadia Matters, 2012.

41 C. B. Corcoran, D. Hess and M. Sweet, Directors, *Occupied Cascadia*. [Film]. Cascadia: Cascadia Matters, 2012.

42 C. B. Corcoran, D. Hess and M. Sweet, Directors, *Occupied Cascadia*. [Film]. Cascadia: Cascadia Matters, 2012.

43 S. McFague, "Toward a New Cascadian Civil Religion of Nature," in *Cascadia: The Elusive Utopia - Exploring the Spirit of the Pacific Northwest*, Vancouver, Ronsdale Press, 2009, pp. 157-172.

44 C. B. Corcoran, D. Hess and M. Sweet, Directors, *Occupied Cascadia*. [Film]. Cascadia: Cascadia Matters, 2012.

45 C. Woodard, American Nations: A History of the Eleven Rival Regional Cultures of North America, New York: Penguin Books, 2011.

46 C. Woodard, American Nations: A History of the Eleven Rival Regional Cultures of North America, New York: Penguin Books, 2011.

47 I. Berlin, "Two Concepts of Liberty," in *Liberty*, New York, Oxford University Press, 1995, pp. 166-217.

48 I. Berlin, "Two Concepts of Liberty," in *Liberty*, New York, Oxford University Press, 1995, pp. 166-217.

49 I. Berlin, "Two Concepts of Liberty," in *Liberty*, New York, Oxford University Press, 1995, pp. 166-217.

50 I. Berlin, "Two Concepts of Liberty," in *Liberty*, New York, Oxford University Press, 1995, pp. 166-217.

51 I. Berlin, "Two Concepts of Liberty," in *Liberty*, New York, Oxford University Press, 1995, pp. 166-217.

52 I. Berlin, "Two Concepts of Liberty," in *Liberty*, New York, Oxford University Press, 1995, pp. 166-217.

53 I. Berlin, "Two Concepts of Liberty," in *Liberty*, New York, Oxford University Press, 1995, pp. 166-217.

54 I. Berlin, "Five Essays on Liberty: Introduction," in *Liberty*, New York, Oxford University Press, 1995, pp. 3-54.

55 T. Jefferson, *Declaration of Independence*, Philadelphia, 1776.

56 I. Berlin, "Two Concepts of Liberty," in *Liberty*, New York, Oxford University Press, 1995, pp. 166-217.

57 J. S. Mill, On Liberty (Re-printed Edition), New York: Dover Publications, Inc., 2002.

58 J. S. Mill, On Liberty (Re-printed Edition), New York: Dover Publications, Inc., 2002.

59   J. S. Mill, On Liberty (Re-printed Edition), New York: Dover Publications, Inc., 2002.

60   J. S. Mill, On Liberty (Re-printed Edition), New York: Dover Publications, Inc., 2002.

61   J. S. Mill, On Liberty (Re-printed Edition), New York: Dover Publications, Inc., 2002.

62   J. S. Mill, On Liberty (Re-printed Edition), New York: Dover Publications, Inc., 2002.

63   J. S. Mill, On Liberty (Re-printed Edition), New York: Dover Publications, Inc., 2002.

64   S. McFague, "Toward a New Cascadian Civil Religion of Nature," in *Cascadia: The Elusive Utopia - Exploring the Spirit of the Pacific Northwest*, Vancouver, Ronsdale Press, 2009, pp. 157-172.

65   S. McFague, "Toward a New Cascadian Civil Religion of Nature," in *Cascadia: The Elusive Utopia - Exploring the Spirit of the Pacific Northwest*, Vancouver, Ronsdale Press, 2009, pp. 157-172.

66   E. De Place, "Coal Exports and Carbon Consequences II," Sightline Institute, Seattle, 2012.

67   E. De Place, "The Northwest's Pipeline on Rails: Crude Oil Shipments Planned for Puget Sound, Grays Harbor, and the Columbia River," Sightline Institute, Seattle, 2014.

68   CBC News, "Northern Gateway Pipeline Recommended for Federal Approval, with Conditions," Canadian Broadcasting Corporation, Toronto, 2013.

69   MSN News Canada, "B.C. Officially Opposes Enbridge Northern Gateway Pipeline," MSN, 2013.

70   RT News, "'Unbelievable Devastation': Massive Mining Waste Spill Causes Water Ban in Canada," Washington, 2014.

71   E. Shogren, "Why the Exxon Valdez Spill Was a Eureka Moment for Science," National Public Radio, Washington, 2014.

72   D. Joling, "25 Years Later, Exxon Valdez Spill Effects Linger," Associated Press, Anchorage, 2014.

73 Bloc Quebecois, "Policy Statement – 2011 Election," Montreal, 2011.

74 Global Footprint Network, "Footprint Basics – Introduction," Oakland, 2010.

75 R. Evanoff, Interviewee, *Building Bioregional Politics for an Ecological Civilization.* [Interview]. 3 August 2012.

76 A. Lincoln, *First Inaugural Address,* Washington, 1861.

77 *Texas v. White - 74 U.S. 700. United States Supreme Court,* 1869.

78 *Texas v. White - 74 U.S. 700. United States Supreme Court,* 1869.

79 *U.S. Const. art. IV, § 3.*

80 *Reference re: Secession of Quebec - 2 SCR 217: 25506. Supreme Court of Canada,* 1998.

81 United Nations General Assembly, *Resolution 1514 (XV) - Declaration on the Granting of Independence to Colonial Countries and Peoples,* New York, 1960.

82 I. Reifowitz, "Liberal Nationalism is Not Only Possible, it's Essential," Daily Kos, 2014.

83 I. Reifowitz, "Liberal Nationalism is Not Only Possible, it's Essential," Daily Kos, 2014.

84 I. Reifowitz, "Liberal Nationalism is Not Only Possible, it's Essential," Daily Kos, 2014.

85 T. Paine, Common Sense (Re-printed Edition), New York: Dover Publications, Inc., 1997.

86 Anonymous, "Onward to Cascadia: Toward a Worker's Ecotopia," *Slingshot,* no. 112, 2013.

87 T. Paine, Common Sense (Re-printed Edition), New York: Dover Publications, Inc., 1997.